NATIONALLY COMPETITIVE SCHOLARSHIPS

Serving Students and the Public Good

THE NATIONAL ASSOCIATION OF FELLOWSHIPS ADVISORS

• 2005 CONFERENCE PROCEEDINGS •

Edited by Suzanne McCray

THE UNIVERSITY OF ARKANSAS PRESS
FAYETTEVILLE
2007

ISBN-10: 1-55728-860-7
ISBN-13: 978-1-55728-860-8

11 10 09 08 07 5 4 3 2 1

Designed by Ellen Beeler

The paper used in this publication meets the minimum requirements of the American
National Standard for Permanence of Paper for Printed Library Materials Z39.48-1984.

Library of Congress Cataloging-in-Publication Data

National Association of Fellowships Advisors. Conference (3rd : 2005 : Louisville, Ky.)
Nationally competitive scholarships : serving students and the public good : The
National Association of Fellowships Advisors 2005 conference proceedings / edited by
Suzanne McCray.
     p.cm.
Includes bibliographical references and index.
ISBN 1-55728-860-7 (pbk. : alk. paper)
1. Scholarships—United States—Evaluation—Congresses. 2. College students—
Scholarships, fellowships, etc.—United States—Congresses. I. McCray, Suzanne,
1956–II. Title
LB2338.N22 2005
371.2'230973–dc22

                        2007019495

Contents

Keynote Address

Essays

Contributors

ADDRESS

Richard J. Light, the Walter H. Gale Professor of Education at Harvard University, teaches statistics and program evaluation, with an emphasis on initiatives in education. He has published seven books; the most recent, *Making the Most of College*, received the Stone Award for the best book on education and society. Others include *Summing Up* (with Judith Singer and John Willett) and *By Design* (with David Pillemer). Light has served as president of the American Evaluation Association, on the national board of the American Association of Higher Education, and on the national board of the Fund for the Improvement of Postsecondary Education. He served as chair of the Panel on American Education for the National Academy of Sciences. He is a Fellow of the American Academy of Arts and Sciences and chairs its project to explore changing demographics in education. At the Kennedy School, Light is chair of a university-wide program called the Young Faculty Leaders Forum, connecting faculty from twenty-four leading American universities to leaders from both business and government.

ESSAYS

Laura Damuth is director of Undergraduate Research and Fellowship Advising at the University of Nebraska–Lincoln. She also has a courtesy appointment in the School of Music and teaches classes in the University Honors Program. She holds a BA from Vassar College, and MA, MPhil, and Ph.D. degrees from Columbia University. Dr. Damuth was hired by the University of Nebraska–Lincoln in 1999 to administer the Undergraduate Creative Activities and Research Experiences (UCARE). Under her guidance, UCARE has grown to nearly 400 undergraduate students working with over 350 faculty members. Her own research interests revolve around the Italian cantata in the seventeenth and eighteenth centuries, most specifically those of Alessandro Scarlatti.

Mary Denyer has been the assistant secretary and head of Scholarship Administration of the Marshall Aid Commemoration Commission for six years. Responsible for the administration of the Marshall Scholarships, a British government sponsored scholarship for Americans, her job ranges from drafting policy for the Foreign and Commonwealth Office to the pastoral care of the 100 Scholars that are in the United Kingdom each year. Ms. Denyer has an international perspective in matters related to education and policy, having worked for the Association of Commonwealth Universities for ten years, the American College in London for three years and as an intern at the Fulbright Commission in London. She has a B.A. (Hons) in American Studies and History from the University College of Ripon and York St. John (University of Leeds) and a PG Dip in Higher and Professional Education from the Institute of Education, University of London. Ms. Denyer is currently a mentor for the Association of University Administrators' Post-Graduate Certificate in Higher Education Administration and also a member of the Marketing Committee for International Education Week. She is also an active participant in the National Association of Fellowships Advisors, where she presents sessions not only on Marshall Scholarships, but also on British education in general.

Bob Graalman grew up in Fairview, Oklahoma, and attended Oklahoma State University (OSU) from 1965 to 1972, earning a master's degree in English, and finishing his education with a Ph.D. in English at the University of Tulsa in 1977. He has taught at Cascia Hall Private School, the University of Tulsa, Illinois State University, and has had an administrative and adjunct teaching career in the Honors College and English Department at OSU since 1981—starting as an assistant to the dean of Arts and Sciences, then director of University Scholarships, and for the last ten years director of Scholar Development and Recognition. He is a founding member of NAFA and served two terms as president, an association that he considers, in addition to working with students, to be his most fortunate, significant, and rewarding professional experience.

Carol Madison Graham holds advanced degrees from Georgetown University in Middle East History and International Relations. She began her involvement in international education as a U.S. diplomat. She moved to London in 1995 with her family where she has worked in the higher education, law, and government sectors. From 2002 to late 2006 she was executive director of the U.S. U.K. Fulbright Commission. During that time she founded the U.K. Scholarship Network for heads of U.K.-based scholarship organizations and was heavily involved in initiatives to increase diversity of institutions and students in scholarships on the United Kingdom, European, and international level. She is currently writing a guide to anti-Americanism for the American study abroad community. Ms. Graham serves on a number of boards including the Carnegie U.K. Trust.

Jane Morris is a 1978 graduate of Villanova University with both a B.S. in Biology and a B.A. in Honors. After receiving an M.A. in Biology from Bryn Mawr College, Jane worked as a research scientist in both the private and public sector for nearly twenty years. In September 2001, she became Villanova's first director of Competitive Grants and Awards. In this capacity, Ms. Morris provides guidance for students applying for nationally competitive scholarships and direction for the Connelly Delouvrier International Scholars Program, the Presidential Scholarship Program, and the Villanova University Undergraduate Student Collaborative Research Awards. In addition, Ms. Morris currently serves as secretary for NAFA. In 2004 and 2006, she directed site visits by NAFA members to universities in the United Kingdom, Ireland, and Northern Ireland.

Joe Schall is a writing tutor and the Giles Writer-in-Residence for Penn State's College of Earth and Mineral Sciences. His books include *Writing Recommendation Letters: A Faculty Handbook* and *Writing Personal Statements and Scholarship Application Essays: A Student Handbook*. His articles have appeared in publications including *Writers' Forum* (U.K.) and *Academe*. He has won numerous awards for his fiction, including an Individual Creative Artists Fellowship in Literature from the Pennsylvania Council on the Arts and the Bobst Award for Emerging Writers from New York University. His short stories have appeared in journals including *The Baltimore Review* and *Indiana Review*.

Camille Stillwell coordinates the National Scholarships Office at the University of Maryland, College Park, which she established in 1999. She is a founding member of the National Association of Fellowships Advisors and was a co-presenter on the topic of International Students and National Scholarships at the 2005 NAFA Conference in Louisville, Kentucky. Ms. Stillwell has served on national selection committees for the James Madison Fellowship, the Jacob Javits Fellowship, and the Orphan Foundation.

Mary Hale Tolar, a Truman Scholar (1988) and a Rhodes Scholar (1989), has established and directed postgraduate scholarship programs at the University of Tulsa and Willamette University, and worked closely with the scholarship programs at George Washington and Kansas State Universities. In early 1999, she began serving as the deputy executive secretary of the Truman Scholarship Foundation and was the first to suggest the possibility of an organization that would have as its membership postgraduate scholarship advisors. She is a founding member of NAFA and was its inaugural Foundation Liaison. She now serves as the associate director for Civic Leadership at Kansas State University.

Tara Yglesias has served as the deputy executive secretary of the Truman Foundation for the past three years and has been involved in the selection of Truman Scholars since 2001. During this time, she had the opportunity to study the trends and characteristics of each incoming class of Scholars. She used this knowledge to assist in the development of new Foundation programs and initiatives as well as the design of a new Foundation website and on-line application system. An attorney by training, she began her career by spending six years in the Office of the Public Defender in Fulton County, Georgia. She specialized in trial work and serious felonies and also assisted with the training of new attorneys. A former Truman Scholar from Pennsylvania, she also served as a Senior Scholar at Truman Scholars Leadership Week and the Foundation's Public Service Law Conference prior to joining the Foundation's staff.

REPORTS

Mark Bauer, associate director of the Office of International Education and Fellowship Programs at Yale University, focuses his fellowship advising on the U.K. and Irish fellowships. He has taught at Yale since 1996—first for the English Language Institute, a summer program for advanced international students, and later for the English Department. He also serves as the writing tutor of one of Yale's residential colleges and is a member of the NAFA board.

Elizabeth Vardaman, associate dean in the College of Arts and Sciences and associate director of the Honors Program at Baylor University, Waco, Texas, has taught at Baylor since 1980. An exchange professor in China and assistant director for several Baylor abroad programs in England and The Netherlands, she has traveled extensively on behalf of the university and led the first NAFA tour of British higher education. Her overview of that trip, "Keys to the United Kingdom," was published in *Beyond Winning: National Scholarship Competitions and the Student Experience*. She has been serving as a scholarship advisor since 1998 and was a charter member of the National Association of Fellowships Advisors. She and Jane Morris (Villanova University) co-chaired the 2006 NAFA Higher Education Symposia, in the United Kingdom and the Republic of Ireland.

Acknowledgements

Conferences and symposia do not just happen. Energetic, dedicated people volunteer their time to create these special events that benefit so many. The planning committee met frequently and committed hundreds of hours collectively to make the Louisville event a success. Special thanks to Mark Bauer, Yale University; Sharon Chambers Gordon, University of Puget Sound; Jane Curlin, Udall Foundation; James Duban, University of North Texas; Susan Kraus Whitbourne, University of Massachusetts–Amherst; Suzanne McCray, University of Arkansas; Beth Powers, University of Illinois at Chicago; John Richardson, University of Louisville; Richelle Stafne, Oklahoma State University; Mary Tolar, Kansas State University; Paula Warrick, American University; Karen Weber, University of Houston, and Gordon Johnson, National Association of Fellowships Advisors (NAFA) liaison. Critical to the success of the conference was the cooperative support of foundation members: Louis Blair, then executive secretary, Truman Scholarship Foundation; Mary Denyer, assistant secretary, Marshall Aid Commemoration Commission; Walter Jackson, program manager, Fulbright U.S. Student Programs; Gordon Johnson, provost, Gates Cambridge Trust; Kristin Kelling, program manager, Morris K. Udall Foundation; John A. Lanning, reader, Goldwater Foundation; Melissa Millage, program assistant, Morris K. Udall Foundation; Richard McGee, director of Student Affairs, NIH Graduate Partnerships Program; Sharon Nichizaki, senior program officer, NSEP David L. Boren Fellowships; Tom Parkinson, Beinecke Scholarship Program; Dell Pendergrast, then director, George Mitchell Scholarship Program; Christopher Powers, deputy director, U.S. Student Programs, Institution of International Education; David Rippon, associate director, Thomas Watson Foundation and J.K. Watson Fellowship; Renee Stephenson, The Rotary Foundation; Peter Storandt, director of Institutional Relations, The Washington Center for Internships and Academic Seminars; Renee Stowell, marketing coordinator, British Counsel U.S.A.;

Elizabeth Veatch, director, NSEP Fellowships and Grants; Joshua Wyner, chief program officer, Jack Kent Cooke Foundation; Tara Yglesias, associate executive secretary, Truman Scholarship Foundation; Paul Yost, director, James Madison Memorial Fellowship Foundation; Michael Cochise Young, director, Scholarship Programs, The Flinn Foundation.

These proceedings also contain reports on the NAFA Higher Education Symposia held in the summer of 2006 in the United Kingdom and Ireland. We greatly appreciate the efforts of Gordon Johnson, president of Wolfson College, Cambridge University, without whom the Cambridge symposium simply would not have happened. Elizabeth Vardaman and Jane Morris served as co-chairs of the symposia planning committee (which included Mark Bauer, Ann Brown, Christopher Howland, Suzanne McCray, John Richardson, Paula Warrick, and Susan Whitbourne). Their leadership kept the committee, and the various universities involved, energized, and on task. Marie Lawlor (International Office) served as our liaison to University College Dublin and was tireless in her support of the events held there.

Special thanks to Richard Light of Harvard for delivering the keynote address in Louisville and to all the presenters at the conference and at the symposia. The support of University of Arkansas Chancellor John White, Provost Bob Smith, and Honors College Dean Bob McMath helped make this publication possible as did the efforts of the University of Arkansas Press team: Larry Malley, director; Brian King, director of editing, design, and production; and Julie Watkins, assistant to the director.

Foreword

In the summer of 2005 at the third biennial conference of the National Association of Fellowships Advisors (NAFA), we honored our roots with the title "Serving Students and the Public Good: Contexts for Fellowship Advising." Prior to 2000 the Truman Foundation, with its legacy of acknowledging the vital role of public servants in our society through its awards, served the scholarship advising community by organizing conferences that allowed us to learn from each other and foundations about how to serve students as they negotiated the award processes. A by-product of these events was discovering the many award winners who had gone on to roles in serving their communities and their fellow humans in a variety of contexts. In addition to well-known scholarship winners like former President Bill Clinton and Supreme Court Justice Stephen Breyer, there are many others working as scientists, lawyers, doctors, activists, educators, and in elected positions. Learning the scope of contributions made by so many who had come through scholarship processes, with and without awards, made a strong impression on me. When I meet intelligent students with ambitious goals and work with them through application processes, I am reminded that our work can help reinforce student commitment to contributing to the public good as they continue their education and eventually embrace careers.

With a great debt to the Truman Foundation, NAFA was officially launched in May 2000 as it became clear to many advisors that despite the competition between us, we all valued the community and opportunity to share what unites us—a desire to help students achieve their goals. We now have a biennial national conference, summer workshops in the off year, an active listserv and bulletin board, and these proceedings. We have also organized three higher education symposia in the United Kingdom with the help of foundations and universities there. NAFA's mission makes it clear that our goal is more than simply encouraging advisors to share:

The purpose of the NAFA is to provide its membership with access to necessary information concerning national undergraduate and graduate grants, scholarships, and fellowships and the foundations that support them, and to provide a format for the exchange of ideas concerning the scholarship process, the foundations, and the ethical issues surrounding the advising process. The long-term goal is to provide information support for faculty and staff who are assisting students through the complex process of applying for these awards.

In these pages, NAFA members and invited guests have addressed the intersection of fellowships and the public good in multiple ways. Dr. Richard Light, author of *Making the Most of College*, shares his findings from college student surveys of satisfaction with college life, enlightening us about what contributes to a positive college experience. Advisors examine important topics in the development of a fellowships office with focus on working with students and faculty members of various backgrounds, and supporting programs as we serve students. Scholarship providers also reflect on the active civic engagement that so many of their scholars embrace. In addition, our United Kingdom trips are detailed by members who organized them. This collection provides important practical information that is beneficial to advisors helping students apply for major awards. It also includes strategies for building a fellowships office, for motivating students to achieve their goals—not simply awards—and ways to involve faculty effectively in the process. These insights into how we and our institutions can better serve students may ultimately lead to our students promoting the public good to the benefit of us all.

Beth Powers, president (2005–2007)
National Association of Fellowships Advisors

Introduction

This volume contains essays and reports sometimes directly, sometimes loosely based on the National Association of Fellowships Advisors (NAFA) conference held in Louisville in 2005. *Serving Students and the Public Good: Contexts for Fellowship Advising* highlighted the public service many of our students engage in before applying for nationally competitive fellowships and their civic involvement as scholars and members of their campus, local, and global communities. Some scholarship programs explicitly seek students whose commitment to civic engagement is long-term and sustained. Truman, Udall, Madison, and Jack Kent Cooke include questions in their applications that make clear their priorities. The Truman Foundation reports on its website that many applications do not advance due to the "lack of a substantial and sustained record of service." The NSF Graduate Research Fellowship application asks applicants to discuss the "broader impacts" of their research plans.

Other scholarships do not require or even specifically inquire about service though they repeatedly select students who have made special contributions beyond the classroom. A quick review of the 2007 profiles of such scholars confirms this: He founded "Georgia PACE, an educational organization aimed towards encouraging civic engagement in young people." She conducted "her senior honors thesis research in Kosovo and New York City, completing a cross-cultural study of current and returned refugee populations." He was "instrumental in establishing the *Global Health Review*, and organizing a world health conference, both of which are intended to focus attention on the inadequacies of health care services in the developing world." "A Fulbright Scholar in China . . . she conducts research on women's rights." He co-founded "the non-profit organization, Reach the World. RTW's mission is to connect underprivileged students to world-travelers on real journeys via the Internet." She has also "interned at the American Cancer Society and worked as a research assistant and hospital volunteer." He has "worked and interned with the Prosecutor General of Rwanda, the International Criminal Tribunal for the Former Yugoslavia, the U.S. Department of Justice, Street Kids of Rwanda, and Tillers International Animal Traction Organization." He is "the founder of an award-winning non-profit organization, Paperclips for Peace in Sudan, which raises funds for Darfur." Such descriptions abound.

All this is not to suggest that service is *the* critical factor in the selection process. Students receiving distinguished scholarships are outstanding scholars in their fields. But there is clearly something very appealing to selection committees (and to advisors) about students who understand the challenges of their communities (local and beyond) and want to commit their expertise and their abundant energies to efforts bringing relief and (when possible) long-range solutions.

We are all concerned with broadening the impact of the work we do. Foundations meet to insure that the broad goals of their scholarship programs are being met. In *Beyond Winning*, Mary Tolar, Alice Ilchman, and Warren Ilchman summarized a meeting of the major foundations in Bellagio, outlining shared goals (italics have been added):

- imparting specific substantive skills and knowledge
- redirecting or raising career objectives
- strengthening leadership skills
- *encouraging public service*
- *increasing international understanding*
- sustaining creativity
- *increasing participation of the underrepresented*
- furthering international mobility
- *developing a global or international perspective or affinity*
- *other public goals* ("Strengthening Nationally Competitive Scholarships")

Clearly, foundations hope to expand the impact of their awards by selecting students committed to public service and by an explicit interest in the broad training these students receive. Foundations articulate service goals of their own, realized through the scholars they select.

The universities that prepare these students are also taking stock, assessing the value of the preparation they provide. As tuition skyrockets to more than $50,000 a year in some cases, those who pay (students, parents, and taxpayers) are demanding that higher education prepare students to not only earn, but also contribute. Universities are seeking ways to determine the wider usefulness of what students are learning and then to expand that learning by putting that knowledge to work in the community. The Higher Education Commission annual meeting in April of 2007 held numerous sessions on assessment. Many universities are embracing ACT's Collegiate Assessment of Academic Proficiency ("The Measure of Learning," *US News and World Report*, March 12, 2007). Service is quickly becoming part of the general education assessment, linking the curriculum to ambitious out-of-classroom experiences popular with today's students. More than 1,100 colleges and universities have used the National Survey of Student Engagement to determine the strength of their programs; institutions use the data "to identify aspects of the undergraduate experience inside and outside the classroom that can be improved through changes in policies and practices more consistent with good practices in undergraduate education" (http://nsse.iub.edu). Student service and learning outside the classroom is becoming an essential "best practice" in higher education. And as Derek Bok points out, it is one way in which our colleges and universities have been underachieving. Recent, sometimes controversial, changes in the Harvard curriculum are directly tied to making learning more relevant to the student and to the global community.

Richard Light, keynote speaker of the Louisville conference, addresses these issues in his essay, "Recognizing and Challenging Our Colleges' Most Outstanding Students." Light himself was challenged by then Harvard President Derek Bok to gain an understanding of what students were learning at Harvard—what Harvard was getting right and what it was not, especially in connection with advising. What Light found from countless interviews was that students who engaged outside the classroom in experiences that complemented their studies were consistently the most successful. He asked students (including those winning Marshall, Mitchell, Fulbright, Rhodes, and Gates Cambridge scholarships) what their main job was, pushing them to evaluate what they hoped to gain from their four years and how they hoped to do it. Light's remarks fit within a context of curricular change occurring at Harvard. In the spring of 2007, Harvard released a report of its task force on general education, announcing that one of the four "overarching goals in linking the college experience to the world its graduates will confront" is preparing them for civic engagement: "Harvard should seek, throughout the college experience and in its general education curriculum in particular, to inspire its students to become active and engaged citizens locally, nationally, and internationally" (http://www. fas.harvard.edu/curriculum-review/general_education.pdf). All of us have been witness to similar changes on our campuses with creation of leadership and service learning programs. Light's advice to advisors—to encourage students to engage and to connect them to faculty mentors and special programs—is critical as we work to broaden the impact of what to do and to expand the institutional definition of winning.

Three essays in this collection specifically point to broadening our definition of winning. Jane Morris' "Alternative Winning" includes profiles of several students she has advised in recent years who have applied for major scholarships as a means to further both educational and service goals. The applications were unsuccessful, but as the title states, the students themselves were quite successful, benefiting from a process that helped them bring in focus and subsequently realize long-term goals. Robert Graalman's essay, "Defining Moments in the Development of a Fellowships Office," discusses alternative winning at the institutional level, where he created a course *Windows to the World*, with many of the same goals listed earlier from the Bellagio report: impart specific substantive skills and knowledge, raise career objectives, encourage public service, increase international understanding, and more. He and his colleagues have also created special research and study abroad opportunities, providing a wider range of "victories" for students at his institution. In "A Path Revealed," Mary Tolar describes a career change that allowed her to expand her efforts to an everwider audience.

Other essays provide practical information on serving students. Laura Damuth, in "Connecting Undergraduate Research with Fellowship Advising," underscores the importance of Light's advice on connecting undergraduates to mentors, providing practical advice on how to do it. Joe Schall's entertaining and helpful essay, on assisting faculty members in their efforts to write effective letters of recommendation, is an excellent resource for any advisor charged with providing faculty (or student) support. Camille Stillwell makes a persuasive case for directing more advising support to international students, a group often seen by fellowship offices as problematic because so many national scholarship competitions are for

U.S. citizens only. Her list of scholarships open to international students is an essential tool for any office serving this population.

Four essays in the collection focus on advising American students when they become the international student. The final three essays of the collection are reports on NAFA trips to the United Kingdom and to Ireland. In his essay, "Why Visit the United Kingdom: Confession of a Journeyman Fellowship Advisor," Mark Bauer highlights the importance of advisors seeing first-hand the institutions they encourage their students to attend, and he provides key insights he gleaned on his initial and subsequent NAFA trips. Elizabeth Vardaman and Jane Morris both report on the NAFA Higher Education Symposia held at Cambridge and University College Dublin. Their essays provide detailed information helpful to anyone advising students considering graduate studies in the United Kingdom or Ireland and who may also be applying for Rhodes, Marshall, Gates Cambridge, Fulbright, and Mitchell Scholarships. And former Executive Director of the U.S./U.K. Fulbright Commission Carol Madison Graham, in her essay, "Student Ambassadors in the Age of Anti-Americanism," reminds advisors that it is not enough to simply connect students to the right program abroad. Students must understand what it means to be an American abroad during an unpopular war; only then can they serve as ambassadors "in this turbulent world of today."

Finally, Mary Denyer, assistant secretary and head of scholarship administration of the Marshall Aid Commemoration Commission, and Tara Yglesias, deputy executive secretary of the Truman Foundation, point to scholars who are not only learning, but also contributing in a variety of ways to the public good, realizing already the initial promise they demonstrated when applying for competitive scholarships.

NAFA is based on partnerships between foundations and institutions, between advisors and students, between students and their communities. The Foundations' Bellagio report stressed, "As citizens in societies, concerned with merit, we believe that talent is broadly, even randomly, distributed, but only selectively developed. . . . We are concerned that we may be missing many qualified individuals, often from groups underrepresented in many ways in our societies. Missing their potential contribution deprives not only them but also us. It seems worthwhile to enlarge the pool even at the expense of having more disappointed people—those worthy but not chosen." NAFA continues to be deeply committed to increasing the numbers of students whose talents are being fully developed. Even as the bar is raised higher and higher and as the competitive pool expands, NAFA is devoted to assisting an ever growing number of worthy students with the goal that they may become highly trained, broadly distributed, and committed to the public good.

Suzanne McCray
University of Arkansas

Institutional Members of NAFA

Executive Board of Directors

Beth Powers, President, University of Illinois-Chicago
Paula Warrick, Vice President, American University
John Richardson, Treasurer, University of Illinois
Jane Morris, Secretary, Villanova University
Gordon Johnson, Liaison to Foundations, Wolfson College, Cambridge

Board Members

Mark Bauer, Yale University
Doug Cutchins, Grinnell College
Mary Engel, Fordham College
Beth Fiori, Cornell University
Paula Goldsmid, Pomona College
Mona Pitre-Collins, University of Washington
Linna Place, University of Missouri-Kansas City
Alex Trayford, Wheaton College
Susan Krauss Whitbourne, University of Massachusetts-Amherst
Debra Young, University of Mississippi

The following institutions are members of the National Association of Fellowships Advisors:

Alma College
American University
Amherst College
Appalachian State University
Arizona State University
Augsburg College
Ball State University
Bard College

Barnard College
Bates College
Baylor University
Bennington College
Binghamton University
Bowdoin College
Brandeis University
Brigham Young University

Brown University
Bryn Mawr College
Butler University
California State Polytechnic
　University, Pomona
California State University, Fullerton
Carnegie Mellon University
Chapman University
Christopher Newport University
City College of New York, CUNY
City University of New York (CUNY)
Claremont McKenna College
Clarion University of Pennsylvania
Clark University
Clemson University
Colgate University
College of Charleston
College of New Jersey
College of St. Benedict/
　St. John's University
College of St. Scholastica
College of the Holy Cross
College of William & Mary
Colorado College
Colorado State University
Columbia College
Columbia University
Concordia College
Connecticut College
Cornell University
CUNY - Brooklyn College
Dartmouth College
Denison University
DePauw University
Dickinson College
Doane College
Duke University
Eastern Illinois University
Elmira College

Elon University
Emory University
Fairmont State College
Florida Atlantic University
Florida International University
Florida State University
Fordham University
Furman University
George Fox University
George Mason University
George Washington University
Georgetown University
Georgia Institute of Technology
Georgia Southern University
Gettysburg College
Grinnell College
Hamilton College
Hampden-Sydney College
Harding College
Hendrix College
Hobart & William Smith Colleges
Holy Family University
Hunter College
Illinois State University
Indiana University
Indiana University of PA
Iowa State University
James Madison University
John Brown University
John Carroll University
Johns Hopkins University
Juniata College
Kalamazoo College
Kansas State University
Kent State University
Kent State University, Stark Campus
Kentucky State University
Lafayette College
Lamar University

Lebanon Valley College

Lehigh University

Louisiana State University

Loyola College in Maryland

Loyola Marymount University

Loyola University New Orleans

Lynchburg College

Manhattan College

Marist College

Maryland Institute College of Art

Massachusetts Institute of Technology

Mercer University

Messiah College

Miami University of Ohio

Michigan State University

Middle Tennessee State University

Middlebury College

Mississippi State University

Missouri State University

Montgomery College

Mount Holyoke College

Muhlenberg College

Murray State University

New Mexico State University

New York University

North Carolina Central University

North Carolina State University

Northeastern University

Northwestern University

Nova Southeastern University

Oberlin College

Occidental College

Oglethorpe University

Ohio Northern University

Ohio State University

Ohio University

Oklahoma City University

Oklahoma State University

Pennsylvania State University

Pepperdine University

Point Loma Nazarene University

Polytechnic University

Pomona College

Pratt Institute

Princeton University

Purdue University

Queens College

Radford University

Reed College

Rice University

Rochester Institute of Technology

Roanoke College

Roosevelt University

Rutgers University

San Francisco State University

Santa Clara University

Seattle University

Seton Hall University

Simmons College

Smith College

South Dakota State University

Southern Illinois University,
  Carbondale

Southwestern University

St. Edward's University

St. John's College, Annapolis

St. John's College, Santa Fe

St. Joseph's University

Stanford University

Stony Brook University

Suny at Buffalo

Swarthmore College

Syracuse University

Temple University

Texas A&M University

Texas Tech University

The Catholic University of America

The Citadel

Trinity College
Truman State University
Tulane University
Union College
United States Coast Guard Academy
United States Air Force Academy
United States Military Academy
University of Akron
University of Alabama
University of Alabama at Birmingham
University of Albany
University of Arizona
University of Arkansas
University of Arkansas at
  Little Rock
University of California, Berkeley
University of California, Davis
University of California, Irvine
University of California, Los Angeles
University of California, San Diego
University of California,
  Santa Barbara
University of Central Florida
University of Chicago
University of Cincinnati
University of Colorado at Boulder
University of Connecticut
University of Delaware
University of Denver
University of Florida
University of Georgia
University of Houston
University of Illinois at Chicago
University of Illinois at
  Urbana-Champaign
University of Iowa
University of Kansas
University of Kentucky
University of Louisville

University of Maryland,
  Baltimore County
University of Maryland,
  College Park
University of Massachusetts Amherst
University of Memphis
University of Michigan, Ann Arbor
University of Michigan, Flint
University of Minnesota, Morris
University of Minnesota, Twin Cities
University of Mississippi
University of Missouri, Columbia
University of Missouri, Kansas City
University of Nebraska, Kearney
University of Nebraska, Lincoln
University of Nevada, Las Vegas
University of Nevada, Reno
University of New Hampshire
University of North Carolina at
  Chapel Hill
University of North Carolina at
  Greensboro
University of North Dakota
University of North Florida
University of North Texas
University of Notre Dame
University of Oklahoma
University of Pennsylvania
University of Pittsburgh
University of Portland
University of Puget Sound
University of Rhode Island
University of Rochester
University of San Diego
University of Scranton
University of South Carolina
University of South Dakota
University of South Florida
University of Southern Mississippi

University of St. Thomas
University of Tennessee
University of Texas at Arlington
University of Texas at Austin
University of Texas at Dallas
University of the Pacific
University of Tulsa
University of Utah
University of Vermont
University of Washington
University of Wisconsin, Madison
University of Wyoming
Ursinus College
Utah State University
Valdosta State University
Valparaiso University
Vanderbilt University
Vassar College
Villanova University
Virginia Commonwealth University

Virginia Military Institute
Virginia Tech University
Wake Forest University
Washington and Lee University
Washington State University
Wayne State University
Wellesley College
Wesleyan University
West Virginia University
Western Carolina University
Western Kentucky University
Westminster College
Wheaton College (MA)
Willamette University
William Jewell College
Williams College
Worcester Polytechnic Institute
Wright State University
Yale University
Yeshiva University

1

Recognizing and Challenging Our Colleges' Most Outstanding Students

RICHARD J. LIGHT

Richard J. Light, the Walter H. Gale Professor of Education at Harvard University, teaches statistics and program evaluation, with an emphasis on initiatives in education. He has published seven books. The most recent, Making the Most of College, *won the Stone Award for the best book on education and society. Others include* Summing Up *(with Judith Singer and John Willett) and* By Design *(with David Pillemer). Light has served as president of the American Evaluation Association, on the national board of the American Association of Higher Education, and on the national board of the Fund for the Improvement of Postsecondary Education. He served as chair of the Panel on American Education for the National Academy of Sciences. He is a Fellow of the American Academy of Arts and Sciences and chairs its project to explore changing demographics in education. At the Kennedy School, Light is chair of a university-wide program called the Young Faculty Leaders Forum, connecting faculty from twenty-four leading American universities to leaders from both business and government.*

I have taught at my wonderful institution, at Harvard, for my entire adult life (since the late 1980s) as a full-time faculty member. I am not a dean; I am not a provost; I am not a chancellor. I did not attend Harvard, but have a regular full teaching load, and interact with the young men and women regularly, advising, and serving on committees. One afternoon I received a phone call from then Harvard president, Derek Bok. He is a very distinguished and wonderful man. I had been doing work in statistics and program evaluation, and President Bok just called and said, "Dick, you and I don't know each other that well, but you've been around here a while, and I've been around here for a while." He was president for over twenty years, and this was the last third of his presidency, and he said, "I've been thinking about a question, and I wonder if you might have an answer. I'm very proud of our university, and in particular, I'm very proud of our college. Nonetheless, you've been around here long enough, and I've been around here long enough that we both know that we could be doing better. Do you know someone who is systematically evaluating and assessing the effectiveness of the many things we do here when it comes to serving and working with our undergraduates?"

I was not expecting his call. I had given the topic zero thought, and so I just simply said in response, "Oh, what an interesting question," but then the serious answer was, "I can't think of anyone." You can probably guess his next question: "Well, actually, that's why I'm calling," and he simply said, "I'd like to invite you, if you're willing to take a leadership role in this, to gather together a group of your colleagues, your faculty colleagues, also a group of administrators, perhaps some student services, student affairs on our campus, perhaps you might even want to involve some students." "Would you be willing to do that, and see if you can get a handle on the answers to these questions? What are we doing well, what are we doing not so well?" And in the end, of course, I said yes.

I went to see him and asked "When you say evaluate how well we are serving our students, do you mean advising?" and he smiled and he said, "Of course, I mean advising, and you and I both know we are pretty good, but we could improve quite a lot." I remember asking "How about classroom teaching?" and "What about the quality of life on campus?" My university is overwhelmingly residential. "Yes, we should look at it," he said. So the end of the story is I gathered together a group of thirty colleagues, student affairs people, the dean of admissions, the dean of first-year students, the dean of our college, various other such folks including people who lead advising and the person who coordinates our national fellowship advising.

I also invited a dozen undergraduates, carefully selected. We made two decisions. First we had to determine how we would gather information from our undergraduates to answer Derek Bok's question. We decided we would interview students, in depth, one on one, for two to three hours each. The first question was answered. How do we get data? In-depth interviews. The second question was how exactly should we get this done? And we decided one of the best ways to do this was to—and I'm going to choose a word intentionally—*use* (and I mean use in its nicest, most constructive, helpful way) our own undergraduates, training them how to interview fellow students, who are strangers in some cases, and paying them for their time as a form of financial aid. In other words, our plan was to *use* students who were receiving financial aid, supporting their efforts and ours. These students, instead of stamping books out for $8 an hour, would be carefully trained and would interviews fellow students. Now more than fifteen years later, we have interviewed over 2,000 students and have an overview that addresses what we are doing right and what could be improved in preparing our students.

As part of that interview process, we include a focus on a special segment of our population—our highest-ability students. I personally interview every single Rhodes and Marshall winner on our campus. Now, obviously we don't have a million every year, but we have a few, just because of the nature of the institution. After fifteen years, we now have over fifty interviews with these highly competitive students, and I want to share with you the results of some of the things we learned. One of the questions that my colleagues and I ask ourselves, and we genuinely didn't know the answer, is whether the students who win Rhodes and Marshalls and Trumans and the Fulbrights would answer certain questions differently from the other 99.7 percent of our students.

So, with that background, my first message is the usefulness of conducting interviews that have very specific, targeted questions for your undergraduates. I have seen a lot of surveys, but most are not in-depth interviews. I want to simply provide five or six of the questions on that questionnaire to give a flavor of the kind of information we are gathering. The original questionnaire is seven pages and includes seventy questions.[1]

Imagine that I am sitting with a student. This is actually a series of questions that we asked at the beginning of the first year to some first-year students, just this past spring: "On a 1–10 scale, where 10 is really great, and 1 is very disappointing, how would you rate your overall academic satisfaction here as you approach the end of your first year? Approximately how many hours a week would you honestly estimate you actually study outside of class? Do you like the way our first-year advising system is organized? If yes, why? If no, why not? Do you have one specific suggestion for how it might be strengthened?"

We also asked, "Is there a single class you took this past year that you would say profoundly affected you in the couple of semesters you've been here? If yes, what was it and more importantly, why was it so profoundly effective? How was it organized?" The purpose of that question is not to identify some instructor by name—I don't care if it is Mr. Smith or Mrs. Jones—that is not the important thing. Of more interest is whether or not students are saying that a certain kind of teaching is especially important to them or especially engaging for them. This is significant, and we would like to know it. We can share that information with many, many faculty colleagues. *Another question:* "Think of the courses you have taken so far. In the process of taking them, can you think of a specific example where the discussions or the readings got you to change your mind about something you consider important in your life?" *Another set of questions:* "As you think ahead to next year, can you identify one specific thing you will do differently on campus because of what you learned from your experience this past year? If you needed a recommendation from a faculty member for a future job, a summer job, an internship, a fellowship, do you have one or more specific people you can go to?" A final question we ask is "If you were sitting one-on-one with the president of the university for a half an hour and the dean of this college, what single constructive change would you propose to make this place even more challenging and exciting for you and people like you?"

From those results, a number of findings emerge. Several are worth mentioning. One of our questions was "What's the best bit of advice you received as a brand new student here at this college?" and "What's the worst bit of advice you got?" But I'm more interested for a moment in the best bit of advice. What we learned from students in response to that question has profoundly affected the way we advise students, and as I have shared this, and as other campuses have begun asking this exact same question, they are finding exactly what we are finding.

Here's an example. What did I used to do five to ten to fifteen years ago when I advised students? Suppose I have here, young Harry or young Sally. What did I used to do? I bet I did just what many advisors would do. I would welcome them. I would ask them what classes they were planning to take? The point is, in the end, I would just tell them about the college, encourage them to work hard. But now here's the new thing I have added. Now, what all advisors on my campus do—and there are a couple hundred of us—is tell the student that we have one final question for them. We ask the student, very clearly and purposefully, "What is your job this first semester and every semester you are here in college? I do not mean your job to earn money because you need the money; I mean what is your job? What do you hope to accomplish?" I do not know how the students on other campuses would answer. But I can tell you how the students on my campus answered. Almost to a person, they give the same response: "Oh, I see what you're getting at." "Remember, what is your job?" Almost to a person, they'll say "Oh, I see what you're asking. My job is to study hard and do well." I, of course, respond, "Sally, you just hit the jackpot. That's a great answer. I hope you do study hard, and I hope you do very well." But, and here's where we've all learned—we advisors—to become quite relentless. "Sally, what's your real job?" And again now, most of the kids think, "Oh, oh, I see now what you're getting at, Professor Light. My job is to engage fully with the many exciting opportunities available on this campus and to give as well as to take." You know, right off the admissions application. I will smile, but respond seriously, "That's an excellent answer, Sally. I hope you do engage in the most serious way, and I hope you do give and not just take."

But again, relentless, I'll ask, "Sally, what's your real, real job?" You can imagine, after a few moments, the kids just give up: "I'm sorry; I don't know what you're getting at, Professor Light." And then I'll say "Sally, your job—please do not forget this—for your entire time here at this college is to be proactive. Screw up your courage if you have to. Make a special effort if you have to. Try to get to know one faculty member reasonably well each term, and have that one faculty member get to know you reasonably well." And it might take screwing up courage a little bit, especially on the bigger campuses. My campus is medium big; there are many campuses in this room two and three times as big as mine, and there are some that are very small, where it is easier. But anyway, I'll turn to the student, the young student, and say, "Just think, if you are willing to make that effort semester after semester by the time you are approaching your senior year, you will have—even if you fail half of the time—you will have three or four faculty members, because you will succeed half the time, who know you a little bit, who can write recommendations, should you choose to apply for a scholarship or fellowship or for graduate school."

How do you think these spectacularly talented first-year Harvard students respond when I say that to them? Get to know a faculty member? This may seem like a no-brainer. We all know that. It is obvious. But the majority of our first-year students at Harvard College, respond "OOOOOOH!" My point is that students are nervous, even the best ones. They're trying to figure out where's the restroom. They just got to campus. Will I be able to succeed at college? Will I be able to make friends? Will I be happy here? Getting to know a faculty member is not number one on their priority list. This is not new to those who have read *Making the Most of College,* but I want to really drum it home because it turns out to be, according to all our interviews, extremely important to encourage students from the outset to get off to a good start. And that means making an effort to get to know some faculty members.

Typically, when I visit a campus or an organization, the folks who invite me are especially concerned about the students who are struggling. Improving retention is the focus. Whereas students applying for nationally competitive scholarships are generally doing very well to extraordinarily and fabulously well. The question is how can we be most constructively helpful to those students. So, I want to focus on a few of those very, very specific results now. First thing I want to share with you is one of the questions we asked our graduating seniors—eight other campuses asked the same question—and we all pretty much found the same thing, but I am going to refer only to the results on my campus—that is where I come to work every day.

Imagine saying to a graduating senior on your campus "think about all your experiences over the past four years (or it may be five or six years) that you have been at this campus. Is there one, formal or informal, inside of class or outside of class, for credit or perhaps not for credit, that especially stands out in your own mind as being extraordinarily important?" That's the question we asked, and we found that our very best students academically, the academic stars, almost to a person, said something along these lines "becoming attached to a faculty member" or some other person—a visiting scholar, a fellow, someone in a laboratory—and "ideally shaping a project with faculty support." It is important to add that almost always that was *not* done for credit. It was done as an extra step. So, again, some might very well say, "Well, we knew that." Others might say, "Well, yes, but it's hard to implement that on a very large campus." We encourage—and I know many other campuses do too—students from the day they arrive to try to become an apprentice to at least one faculty member. The step that is often left out, and the step that is worth telling students, including star students, whether they are first years students or juniors or seniors, and that step is get to know something about what the faculty member is doing before approaching them.

I would like to give you an example from my own life. Just this past year, the second day of school, a young man showed up at my door and asked if he could make an appointment to see me. I had never heard of him; I had never seen him; I didn't know his name. And it happened I had a few minutes free and invited him to come in. He was obviously very shy and very nervous. He was a new, young, first-year student, just arrived at my college, and he said, "Professor Light, I have looked at your website. I read what you do—interviewing undergraduates—and I think I would like to do that because I'm interested in science, and I would love to understand how to succeed in science at a very complicated place like this university."

Though it was a great offer, I did not know the student and was not sure he would be a good interviewer. And then with his hands almost shaking, he handed me two pages and said, "I printed out my CV, just to give you a sense of my background." So to be polite, I took the CV. I thought it was a joke. There were seventeen papers in refereed scientific journals. I could not understand the titles of most of the papers. Looking at this and then at him, I said "Have you really done this?" And he responded, "Yes." And I said, "You're hired." He helped with many of these questions. It is an entertaining little story, but the real point is this young man did his homework, and that is why I hired him. Sure, he is impressive with his publications (nobody comes to college with seventeen publications), but more importantly he did his homework, and I appreciated it. And it turns out he has been one of the very best interviewers.

The students who have apprenticed themselves to a faculty member often turn out to be the best students, those with the most initiative, and those who in the end faculty members make the biggest investment in, not because we are coaching them to win a Rhodes or a Marshall or a Truman or one of the others, but rather, because they are terrific as research assistants and have the potential to make a real contribution. But I want to let such students speak for themselves. First one: "In a classroom situation, you are the only one who suffers if the work is not your best work. You submit a paper; it is an academic exercise. The professor gives you the assignment. You do the assignment. The professor grades it. But, now for the first time, I had a chance to create my own project, and I realized how hard it was. You treat each step a little bit differently."

Second student: "I think being this junior partner to my professor has really led me to think about my writing in a different way. I'm doing interviews as part of the work, and my obligation is to write up in-depth interviews. My senior partner has stressed the importance of clarity in the writing and the importance of communicating the information well, especially when I've interviewed someone, and I know that I'm responsible to them, as well as to my senior partner. It's great to be motivated by something other than a grade."

Now finally a young student who talks about her mentor: "The best part has actually been having a role model. I know that sounds invariably cheesy, but it is so true, particularly because my senior partner is ten years older than me. So it's been great to have someone who's right between me and my mother. And it has been inspiring to me that in the ten short years this woman has really gotten her act together and is contributing to knowledge. I had no idea how a scientist—she is a biologist—can agonize over practically every word in her project write-ups. Maybe I should have known it, but the fact is I didn't. It completely changed the way I think about my own writing. I've come to enjoy working at it, and it been an unending effort, which I have no doubt will continue."

Well, I obviously could provide many more examples. It takes quite a lot of convincing of faculty on any campus, including mine—to get professors to spend more time working with students and different campuses may or may not reward professors for doing it. I do this as part of my research. Many of my colleagues are thrilled to have talented students helping them. Some campuses will pay students to do it; some will not.

I've supervised a number of research projects, and some of my faculty colleagues have supervised a number of research projects to try to understand specific aspects of student life. And it turns out that the students who have volunteered to do these projects—I emphasize the word volunteered—are precisely the students who are the most likely to be the strongest candidate for nationally competitive scholarships and fellowships. The students who engage succeed. Our job is to provide the opportunities for them to engage.

2

Connecting Undergraduate Research Programs with Fellowship Advising

LAURA DAMUTH

Laura Damuth is director of Undergraduate Research and Fellowship Advising at the University of Nebraska–Lincoln. She also has a courtesy appointment in the School of Music and teaches classes in the University Honors Program. She holds a B.A. from Vassar College, and M.A., M.Phil. and Ph.D. degrees from Columbia University. Dr. Damuth was hired by the University of Nebraska–Lincoln in 1999 to administer the Undergraduate Creative Activities and Research Experiences (UCARE). Under her guidance, UCARE has grown to nearly 400 undergraduate students working with over 350 faculty members. Her own research interests revolve around the Italian cantata in the seventeenth and eighteenth centuries, most specifically those of Alessandro Scarlatti.

A few years ago, I was approached by Rita Kean, dean of Undergraduate Studies at the University of Nebraska–Lincoln (UNL) and asked if I would be interested in serving as the Fellowship Advisor for highly competitive national and international scholarships. I had overseen the university's undergraduate research program, UCARE (Undergraduate Creative Activities and Research Experiences) for several years, and I was coming into contact regularly with highly successful and academically engaged students. Although scholarship advising had been going on at UNL for many years, it had never been centralized in a single office, and with the creation of a new Office of Undergraduate Studies, this seemed a good time to make the shift to a more centralized fellowship advising system.[1]

What I have discovered in the four years that I have been advising for fellowships is that there is a great synergy between the two positions that I hold—more than I would have imagined when I first became a fellowship advisor. Undergraduates involved in research are naturally drawn to the opportunities provided by national scholarships and fellowships, and conversely, the most consistently successful scholarship and fellowship applicants are those who have included undergraduate research as part of their university experience. Since the creation of the UCARE research program and the centralization of all fellowship activity into one office, over 98 percent of the university's postgraduate scholarship applicants have had undergraduate involvement with research.

Not all of us can wear two "hats," and there are times of the year when I am just a little overwhelmed, but if there is an office of undergraduate research on campus or a group of faculty who are regularly working with undergraduates on research, fellowships advisors would do well to partner with them. The popularity of these undergraduate research programs has been steadily on the rise at universities and colleges in the United States over the past ten years. As a result there is an increasing number of undergraduate research program directors. For example, at the Reinvention Center national meeting in College Park, Maryland, in 2002, a gathering of undergraduate research program directors drew about thirty to thirty-five attendees. Just two years later the same conference in Washington, D.C. drew about 150. Additionally the Council on Undergraduate Research (CUR), an organization supporting and promoting undergraduate research, has recently created a new internal division—one for undergraduate research program directors. The emphasis on student research is also evident in this spring's Association of American Colleges and Universities (AACU) conference in Long Beach entitled *The Student as Scholar: Undergraduate Research and Creative Practice.*

Put simply, a well-developed undergraduate research program places students in a position to be extremely competitive for national scholarships. Engaging in research can be extremely beneficial to students as they gain an opportunity to explore a discipline by gaining hands-on experience and skills. Their involvement in research can help prepare them professionally, personally, educationally, and vocationally to take the next step whether it is the job market, graduate school, or fellowship application. Let me describe the UCARE program at the University of Nebraska–Lincoln in more detail to help illustrate what I mean.

From its inception, the administrators at the University of Nebraska–Lincoln wanted an undergraduate research program that was campus-wide, cutting across all disciplines. This has, by necessity, resulted in the UCARE Program developing a relatively broad and inclusive definition of undergraduate research, spanning creative projects in the arts to research service learning in the community. UCARE is designed as a two-year program. It is formative in concept because, during the first year, the student works as a research assistant for a faculty member on the faculty member's ongoing research or creative activity, learning the research methods and techniques of the discipline. By establishing closer ties to faculty, students gain knowledge of what faculty do besides teach. Their learning is also personalized—it is deeper and more comprehensive. It is this "training year" that has been critical in attracting faculty and student participation from a wide variety of fields. Indeed, over fifty percent of the projects funded by UCARE have been outside of the traditional laboratory sciences in such diverse fields as architecture, art and art history, music, history, English, and textiles.

In the first year, the student engages in "learning by doing"—learning why and how the faculty member does research and creative activities by assisting the faculty in completing research tasks. The student may learn such skills as how to do library literature reviews, write code, or retrieve data, work in a research laboratory or historical archive, undertake research techniques specific to a project or discipline, assist with an experiment, or work in an art studio. In the second year the student advances to a more independent project proposed by the student and sponsored by the faculty mentor with whom the student worked during the first year. The project may be an extension of or related to the student's UCARE experience during the first year or may simply build upon skills gained in the first year.

The key factor is that the faculty member sponsors and serves as a mentor for the project. Students working with faculty for two years can receive extremely strong letters of recommendation.

There are at least *three ways* in which overseeing an undergraduate research program or being connected to a program can be directly beneficial to a fellowship advisor: The program identifies students who are eligible for scholarships that require research, the program itself provides opportunities to recruit students for the scholarship office, and the program directly connects the office to faculty.

Scholarships Requiring Research Experience

As we know, certain scholarships require a research component—most notably the Goldwater, the National Science Foundation Graduate Fellowship, or the Fulbright. The only students who will be competitive for these are those who are actively engaged in research (and the more research the better). Students who have been in Nebraska's UCARE program and have experienced two years of a sustained research experience with a single faculty member are well-prepared to take that research to the next level. A high percentage of UCARE students do work in the STEM disciplines, and are therefore, perfect candidates for the Goldwater or NSF Graduate Fellowship. An example is one of our recent Goldwater recipients, who has been actively conducting biomedical research focusing on gene expression as it relates to human disease. She is a UNL Honors student majoring in biochemistry, who has been in UCARE for the past two years. She started working in a biochemistry lab her freshman year, became involved in the UCARE program in her sophomore year, and successfully completed her Goldwater application in her junior year.

Because UCARE is not limited to any particular discipline, UCARE students are also competitive for the Fulbright. For example, a political science student completing his senior honors thesis on "The Recognition of Universal Human Rights in the People's Republic of China" went to the University of Manchester on a Fulbright to complete a master's in human rights. Another student, majoring in history, wrote a senior thesis on Charles Hodge, the principal of Princeton Theological Seminary in the mid-nineteenth century, and is currently at the University of Gottingen on a Fulbright pursuing independent research on Hodge's correspondence with Friedrich August Tholuck, an important conservative German Protestant.

Programmatic Components

Because I have a database of over 350 students who are currently working with faculty on research, I can easily send out reminders of events, workshops, and upcoming deadlines. At UCARE events held throughout the academic year, I remind students of scholarship opportunities. For example, at our annual fall orientation for students entering into the UCARE program, students are given a folder providing basic information on UCARE as well as information sheets on various scholarships along with a letter encouraging them to speak with me. As director of Undergraduate Research I am also frequently invited to speak about UCARE at student clubs: pre-health, psychology, biology, chemistry, biochemistry, and special interest groups. If I am invited to speak about undergraduate research, I always mention my other "job" so that students know that I am an available resource for them.

Establishing a Relationship with Faculty

A key factor in recruiting students for scholarships is faculty involvement. Probably one of the most significant benefits of being both the scholarship advisor and the director of an undergraduate research program is that I have built strong relationships with those faculty members who have been willing to mentor and advise undergraduates on research. To date UCARE has had over 500 different faculty sponsors, representing about one-third of the university's faculty. Faculty who work closely with students can help to differentiate those who do well from those who have that special "spark." They help me in identifying those students who might be competitive. In a sense, then, these faculty members operate like delegates within the department, suggesting to students that they come and visit with me.

Ultimately we also need faculty to help with the process by serving on review committees or mock interview committees. Again, having forged relationships with faculty through the research program, I find these research mentors become great allies in reading and commenting on the applications, helping to select the best applicants to put forward, and, of course, participating in numerous practice interviews throughout the year.

Although my two different positions can make me somewhat schizophrenic at times, ultimately I am grateful for the opportunity to work with students both in setting up research opportunities, and, for some of them, to advise them as they take their experiences here at the university and compete for national fellowships.

3

Marshalling Service

MARY DENYER

---

*Mary Denyer has been the assistant secretary and head of Scholarship
Administration of the Marshall Aid Commemoration Commission for six
years. Responsible for the administration of the Marshall Scholarships, a
British government sponsored scholarship for Americans, her job ranges
from drafting policy for the Foreign and Commonwealth Office to
the pastoral care of the 100 Scholars that are in the U.K. each year.
Ms. Denyer has an international perspective in matters related to
education and policy, having worked for the Association of
Commonwealth Universities for ten years, the American College in
London for three years and as an intern at the Fulbright Commission in
London. She has a B.A. (Hons) in American Studies and History from
the University College of Ripon and York St. John (University of Leeds)
and a PG Dip in Higher and Professional Education from the Institute of
Education, University of London. She also spent a semester at the
University of South Florida, where she was placed on the dean's list for
outstanding students. Ms. Denyer is currently a mentor for the Association
of University Administrators' Postgraduate Certificate in Higher Education*

Administration and also a member of the Marketing Committee for International Education Week. She is an active participant in the National Association of Fellowships Advisors, where she presents sessions not only on Marshall Scholarships, but also on British education in general.

"*A close accord between our two countries is essential to the good of mankind in this turbulent world of today, and that is not possible without an intimate understanding of each other.*" These words appear at the top of the Marshall Scholarship website and come from a letter that General George C. Marshall wrote to the first class of Marshall Scholars in 1954. He went on to say: "*These Scholarships point the way to the continuation and growth of the understanding which found its necessity in the terrible struggle of war years.*"

His message continues to have relevance today, and current Marshalls still exemplify this continuation of understanding, not only through their interaction within the academic programs of the British universities they attend or through the social side of their experience, but also through the actions they take to improve their communities both at home and abroad.

Marshall Scholars arrive in the United Kingdom with an already impressive commitment to service. Some have worked in their home communities and others have spent summer vacations working in developing countries. One of the many challenges they face is to find opportunities to continue this work in a new country, expanding their experiences. In 2001 Ari Alexander, 2001 Scholar, set up the Marshall Scholars Volunteer Project, MSVP, which is a database of volunteering opportunities within the United Kingdom and is kept on the Marshallscholarship.org website.[1] In addition since 2002 Marshall Scholars have also worked on *class projects*, which have fostered a further connection between class members as well as helping enormously in their chosen area.

Community service and volunteering among the recent Marshall classes has fallen roughly into three areas: local community service in all sectors, overseas development activity, and the development of groups for the service of the greater understanding between the United States, the United Kingdom, and Europe.

Local Community Service and Volunteering

Local community work is the most common form of service undertaken by Marshall Scholars in the United Kingdom. Sometimes Scholars will bring interests with them; for example, there is an active group involved with Amnesty International, working with the local groups in the United Kingdom, sometimes leading them and in some cases setting them up. Other Scholars join established volunteering projects at their universities, and others will find opportunities outside the university. The range of projects is impressive with Scholars working with local schools, tutoring undergraduates, working in museums, working on help lines, and assisting deprived members of local communities. Their experiences help not only the recipients of their efforts, but also the Scholars better understand the community and culture that they are living in.

The following statements from the Scholars themselves make this clear as they talk about some of their experiences and the areas they chose to work in:

> *Since arriving in England, I've taken up volunteering each week at the Gatehouse "homeless café" in central Oxford. We provide sandwiches, soup, cakes, hot tea and coffee to any and all in need, and I've had the pleasure of getting to know many of our hundred odd guests, both at the Gatehouse and on the streets of Oxford. The aim is to provide good food and warm drinks in a caring non-judgemental setting, where hungry folks can come in off the streets and stay a while to chat, pick up clothing, check their email, or write and paint. This winter we released our first newsletter* Gateway, *containing the art and poetry of many of our guests, with help from Oxford University Press. Those afternoons have afforded me a wonderful, and more complete, perspective on this city I now call home, and through it I have found many fine friends among the fellow volunteers and guests.*
>
> —Dan Weeks 2006

> *I spent two of my three years in Britain volunteering at the British Museum. I joined the museum's object handling team for an exhibit on British archaeology, which involved helping visitors handle and interpret archaeological specimens. For a year and a half, I assisted Judy Rudoe, the Curator of Modern Collections and Assistant Keeper of the Department of Prehistory and Europe. I digitized the collection of Victorian tiles, meaning that I upgraded and created database entries, photographed the tiles, and uploaded the images to the database. For my dissertation for my Master's degree in*

Victorian Media and Culture, I conducted research on a designer repre-sented in the collection. I also volunteered at the Leighton House Museum cataloguing objects in the museum store. Finally I worked as a volunteer at the Foundling Museum, helping visitors interpret the collections of the Foundling Hospital.

—Laura Gardner 2003

I have started tutoring at my college. St Antony's is the most international college in Oxford and many students have difficulty with writing in English. Generally, these students speak and read proficiently, but have trouble writing in natural English syntax. So, I help with the college tutoring by sitting down with those who need help for two hours each Wednesday night. We go over a short piece of writing to find common errors they can fix in their writing in the future.

—Tom Isherwood 2006

The most notable thing that I did while I was at Oxford was to help orga-nize and perform in the Vagina Monologues. *This was done to raise aware-ness of the continuing dangers of violence against women. All profits were donated to charity, some going to local groups in Oxford, and some going to support the efforts to fight violence against women internationally. Our show sold out—we had about 200 people in the audience, including several highly ranked members of the university—so we made a good amount of money.*

—Talia Karim 2001

Oxford has certainly lived up to its reputation as a great place to get involved with human rights advocacy. Since arriving here last term, I've been volunteering with a variety of rewarding campaigns focused on the rights of refugee asylum seekers, from Amnesty International to Asylum Welcome (a community-based charity that helps asylum seekers, particu-larly young people, access food, health care, and basic legal services). Because the university campus is located nearby Campsfield House Immigration Removal Centre, I've been able to teach a weekly volunteer creative writing class to detainees. I feel as if I'm learning at least as much as the detainees themselves—particularly since the class presents the op-portunity to engage with people from incredibly diverse backgrounds and virtually all corners of the world, from Angola to Afghanistan. I'm also enjoying the chance to engage with refugees in a one-on-one setting as a participant in Asylum Welcome's visitor aid project. This work has only heightened my awareness of the grave political crises many of the refugees face in their home countries, and thus, I've also become active in student awareness campaigns surrounding issues such as the genocide in Darfur. As a member of Hands Up for Darfur, I am working with other Marshall

Scholars and Oxford students to coordinate local educational initiatives about the crisis as well as a national day of student action planned for March 9th. This has been a wonderful way to meet other students concerned with asylum seekers' rights, as well as to learn more about the relationship in our globalized era between local grassroots service projects and broader campaigns for human rights abroad.

—Sarah Stillman 2006

It is clear that the Scholars get a great deal out of these projects and are giving back in a generous manner with their time, experience, and enthusiasm. They are learning about the United Kingdom, the good and the bad. One Scholar who had been volunteering with a Catholic group that helps refugees was shocked to discover that some immigrants were kept in detention centers, and this drove him to find out more about immigration in the United Kingdom and the politics around the immigration and political asylum, and it has also made him think about the policies back in the United States.

By working in their communities, the Scholars also integrate with British volunteers and perhaps learn something about the country they are living in beyond their academic experiences and contact with students.

Overseas Development Activity

Many Scholars come to the United Kingdom having already worked on and sometimes instigated projects that help developing countries. Two significant projects that Scholars have recently worked on are the 2002 class project "Marshall Scholars for the Kigali Public Library" and the 2004 project "Millat School Development Fund." These projects combined fundraising with direct action and gave the classes the opportunity to work for a common cause.

The suggestion for a class project came from Zach Kaufman, 2002 Scholar, who had already been working on a project for the Kigali library in the United States which was an established non-profit. He brought the idea to the class, and they thoroughly supported it. This project aimed to build a public library in Kigali, Rwanda, which would symbolize the rebuilding of the Rwandan society after the genocide in 1994. The project, which is still active, had a broad range of activities that involved most of the class members. The first assignment was fund raising and to date the Marshall class, together with the American Friends of the Kigali Public

Library, has raised $1.4 million. The Marshall class solicited grants from various donors in the United Kingdom and held several very successful fundraising events including a recital at Rhodes House, University of Oxford and a Rwandan film festival hosted at Magdalen College, Oxford.

The Scholars also focused on raising public awareness about the project, and Scholars were involved in writing articles for a range of publications and speaking at various events and conferences. They solicited press coverage in *Newsweek, Voice of America,* the *ACU Bulletin,* and of course the *Marshall Update,* and they spoke to Rotary groups in the United Kingdom and United States, the International Youth Assembly of the YMCA-YWCA Conference, and various United States universities.

The final aspect of the project was learning first-hand about the challenges faced in Rwanda. A group of Scholars traveled to Rwanda in the summer of 2004. They visited genocide sites with survivor groups, met with government officials and civil society organizations, and conducted literacy and education programs at local schools. This trip had a profound effect on the Scholars. The children they met really brought home the impact the genocide had had on the whole country, and this has meant that the Scholars have remained committed to the project beyond the end of their scholarship.

The 2004 class chose to help a school in Nagpur, India. The Millat School Development Fund was proposed by Sameer Ahmed, 2004 Scholar, and aimed to help the Millat School, which is the only educational institution available to poor Muslim children in the area. The class had to create a strategy including establishing the project as a 501(c)3 in the United States. They needed to research the education system in India, set up a bank account, and create a website. They aimed to raise money for the school as well as collect books for the children and also establish a cross-cultural exchange between the school in India and schools in the United Kingdom and United States.

The Scholars between them achieved much of this, and some of the class traveled to India to visit the school, the children, teachers, and the community. This, like the class who traveled to Rwanda before them, really had a major impact on the Scholars; the poverty they saw drove them to push ahead with the project. One of the Scholars filmed the visit and created a piece, which they now use for fund-raising purposes. This film put a human face on the poverty that the children lived in and overcame at least part of the suspicion that some felt about funding a Muslim school. To date the class has raised $60,000 and has donated hundreds of books.

In addition Scholars are hoping to create exchange programs that aim to pair British and American schools with the Millat School allowing the children at the schools in India, the United Kingdom, and the United States to learn about each other and perhaps sometime in the future visit each other.

Both these projects are examples of the energy Marshall Scholars harness in dealing with difficult issues. Their enthusiasm has inspired others, including scholars from other scholarship programs, to involve themselves in these projects.

On a more individual basis, Scholars have also been involved in setting up a non-profit group called Orphans Against Aids, whose mission is to break the cycle of HIV/AIDS by ensuring that all children orphaned and made vulnerable by HIV/AIDS receive a high-quality education. Scholars have also worked with NGO and with UNESCO projects, demonstrating a commitment to helping those less fortunate than themselves. They have used their positions as Marshall Scholars to help further the projects' objectives.

Service for a Greater Understanding Between the U.K. and the U.S.

The Marshall Commission also encourages their Scholars to become not only ambassadors for the United States, but also ambassadors for the United Kingdom. Many Scholars are involved in groups that promote a better understanding between the United States and the United Kingdom.

Formally the Commission has set up a Marshall Scholars' Speakers Program; this allows Scholars to travel to various universities and other interested groups to speak about issues in the United States. Participation in the program is completely voluntary, but most Scholars want to take part. In the last six months Scholars have spoken on "The Phenomenon of Creationism," "Historical and Political Perspectives of the Vietnam War," "Ramifications of the Mid-Term Elections on U.S. Foreign Policy," "Historical Perspectives of American Literature," and more. This program was created in 2000 to help explain the U.S. presidential elections to the British public. It has now developed into a form of debate, explaining various key issues in the United States. In the lead-up to the 2008 presidential elections, the demand for our Scholars should rise, and they will have the opportunity to speak to a diverse cross-section of the British public.

The very experience of studying overseas can open the Scholars' eyes not only to the differences in culture in the country they are studying in, but also to the way the United States is perceived within that culture. Members of the 2001 Marshall class were so concerned about misconceptions both in the United Kingdom and most especially in the United States, that they created Americans for Informed Democracy (AID). In the words of Seth Green, president of AID:

Americans for Informed Democracy was started by a group of Marshall Scholars who studied abroad just after the September 11th attacks. The students were traumatized by September 11th and wary of being overseas so soon after the tragedy. But to their surprise, they were met with intense sympathy and solidarity from people from around the world. For them, the tragedy seemed to reveal the possibility for a global community of shared values.

But when these young Americans came back to the United States, they were often greeted with questions like "How is it living abroad where people hate America?" The students realized that the picture of the rest of the world that Americans were seeing in U.S. media was not the experience of the world that they were living abroad. As an example, these young Americans abroad were having conversations with moderates from the Muslim world about how the United States could work with moderates to help root out extremism. But the only question being asked in the United States at the same time was "who are the extremists and why do they hate us?" The result was that Americans only saw the extremists and threats from around the world and not the collaborative opportunities and potential global partners.

Over time, much of the goodwill that initially embraced the American students abroad vanished and their international peers began raising the question: "Why should the international community support the United States if the United States is not willing to join the international community?" And so, on both sides, misperceptions and stereotypes grew, and the common ground and values that once seemed obvious loomed distant.

These students set up Americans for Informed Democracy to bring the world home to Americans and to showcase the opportunities for the United States to play a more collaborative role in the world from ending global poverty to acting as stewards of our earth. They began hosting town hall forums to bring new questions to the U.S. public. They also hosted international videoconferences that allowed Americans to talk face-to-face with peers from around the world. Based on their own experiences abroad, they believed that if Americans had new ways to connect with the rest of the world, they would see new opportunities for the United States to work with other countries to solve global problems. These students did not seek to advocate a specific position or partisan ideology. Instead, they believed that if Americans just had a chance to be exposed to new issues and new perspectives, and to see the world in terms of both threats and opportunities, they would become more likely to support a collaborative U.S. foreign policy. In other words, they sought to inspire a more informed democracy.

—Seth Green 2001

This group works with students all over the United States and to date the members have brought together 45,000 students for videoconferences and have received media coverage from a wide range of publications, from the *New York Times* to *Marie Claire*.

This type of service is very different to the local community and developing world service as it comes out of the Scholars' experiences overseas. It is encouraging that the Scholars feel so strongly about the issues confronting our societies that they are willing to set up this type of group to try and make a difference.

Marshall Scholars, by their very nature, are people who wish to be engaged, whether locally or globally. Over the years Scholars have been engaged in many types of service activities —this is just a snapshot. It is a tribute to the Scholars that they manage to be involved in so many things and still maintain strong academic performances. In a world where there is so much talk about apathy among the youth, it is encouraging that these future leaders are already so engaged. They demonstrate that the vision of General Marshall and the British government is as relevant today as it was in 1953 when the scholarships were established.

4

Defining Moments in the Development of a Fellowships Office

ROBERT GRAALMAN

Bob Graalman grew up in Fairview, Oklahoma, and attended Oklahoma State University from 1965 to 1972, earning a master's degree in English, and finishing his education with a Ph.D. in English at the University of Tulsa in 1977. He has taught at Cascia Hall Private School, the University of Tulsa, Illinois State University, and has had an administrative and adjunct teaching career in the Honors College and English Department at OSU since 1981—starting as an assistant to the dean of Arts and Sciences, then director of University Scholarships, and for the last ten years director of Scholar Development and Recognition. He is a founding member of NAFA and served two terms as president, an association he considers, in addition to working with students, to be his most fortunate, significant, and rewarding professional experience.

Recently some NAFA officers and founders met in Fayetteville to do a little work and reminisce a lot. Many of you recall that our first opportunity to exchange ideas and formulate plans for what became NAFA occurred in Razorback country in 1999. "Breaking the Code" it was called, and we were inspired by Nancy Twiss, fascinated with each other's problems (we'd thought we were all alone), entertained by our UA hosts, and led by several Marshall and Truman visionaries. Out of that meeting came a Chicago founders' gathering the following spring, and then . . . no need to continue with a historical recounting, I'm sure. Let's just say what has occurred since has transformed the way we deal with our students, affected the way foundations design their programs and communicate with us, and shaped the way we approach our exciting careers—sustaining us even when things might career from one result to another in the blink of an eye, leaving us exhilarated or frustrated, depending on the circumstance, or just plain confused. All this has brought about an explosion of administrative innovations and changes that could not have been anticipated when we began to work together. The ten-year anniversary of NAFA is soon to be on us, and we tinker with our programs and evaluate what works best in our various circumstances.

At our little reunion, we talked about defining moments for NAFA and our schools, and driving home late that night, I ran through a list of events and programs that supporters and participants, on campus and off my own campus, would cite as fulfilling our administrative mission. First-time winners of major awards or multiple winners by a single person come to mind as obvious examples, especially if alumni or media had a say. Of course, in these cases it has been my solemn duty to remind everyone what we are really trying to do is provide more opportunities for more students in a general educational context. I would point out that we have gradually increased the number of students applying, so what used to be an annual "count" of eight to ten candidates/nominees each year has increased now to forty to fifty annually. "That's not bad at a land grant school on the plains," I am always careful to emphasize to the upper administration—especially when "wins" might be few and far between in any given year. Tempering expectations—for students, faculty, and administrators—is important in the fragile world of scholarship advising.

I then thought about how we embrace good ideas "back home," especially in regard to the listserv reports we receive and what we learn at conferences. Truly, have you ever seen a group of more enthusiastic note-takers and questioners than our colleagues at any given NAFA session? "Will that work at my school?" is the unspoken subtext for us all, and we all have enjoyed various fantasies—("If only we had their funds," "Look at the support that program has from its administration," "Ten qualified Rhodes candidates? What I could do with all of them!"). And then we remind ourselves of the rare qualities of our own students and resources and support that we enjoy perhaps not available elsewhere.

I'm reminded of a conversation with a student several years ago who came to see me after reading about our first multiple winner, an "academic double-play" I called it at the time (rare then, but not so much now, thanks to NAFA). This was a Marshall and Truman for one of the best candidates I've ever known; you know the type, does everything himself, never saw a comma splice he could not fix, holds off on telling you he's won anything because it would be bragging (in other words a perfect gem of a person). Anyway, after some small talk, I asked this new student what I could do for him, and he said "I'd like to see John's resume to find out what he did during the summer after his sophomore year; if it worked so well for him it might for me too, and I do not have any plans yet." This led to a long and heartfelt talk about motivation and preparation, emphasizing the importance of understanding "self" as the primary factor in any such endeavor, and not trying to become someone else.

I was inspired last year when I began to see detailed syllabi for those terrific training courses many of us have developed for prospects who might eventually become viable candidates. I felt a little unsettled over my own efforts when I saw the careful planning and brilliant organization that many had brought to the task—books ordered, lectures planned, and weekly goals set. Why? Maybe I'm just making excuses for my own lack of organization, but in my course, "Windows to the World," which started with seven earnest students nearly twelve years ago and now has two sections of sixteen every spring, I've never planned a thing or ordered a text. It's my gift to the bright students whose every move these days is already dictated by syllabi and schedules, goals and objectives. We talk about the news; we challenge each other if the reasoning's not quite right. We look at several major scholarship programs and try to find the right fit, and then we talk more until we've had enough. I have no idea what I'm supposed to accomplish in that class, except to entertain them a little, supply some pointers on debate and writing skills, and let them experience—perhaps for the first and probably last time in their educational lives—a totally unstructured, but guided afternoon of stimulating conversation with peers. My only responsibility is to make them squirm a little from time to time when their comments are off target, they dangle a modifier, or they struggle with plural/singular usage of phenomena/phenomenon, and to be supportive and nonjudgmental in so doing. Again—that's what works for us in Stillwater, and I'm sure all those new courses are doing similar things on countless different campuses.

Is it any wonder there are so many different structural models and reporting lines for our work, which I recall was one of the first formal studies undertaken after NAFA's founding? The evolution of "scholar development" offices on our campuses has wandered in so many directions that future reports on the myriad arrangements will be lengthy. But for us in NAFA, what we imagine, what our students need, and what our superiors expect have generated some creative solutions perhaps unmatched in higher education recently.

I feel grateful that unplanned, even serendipitous opportunities have become staples of our offerings here. A foundation that had long served our school with loans and work study decided to change directions a decade ago, wanting to focus on undergraduate research and leadership opportunities at highly competitive levels. Ten years later we give 100 leadership scholarships, the largest of its type on campus, to undergraduates, and more importantly (in my view), fifty research scholarships to students who want to engage in professional-level experiences in their fields, working with a faculty research mentor, making connections on our campus and across the globe. I am convinced that program is the most important and useful of anything we do here, and the majority of the hundreds of students I've worked with during the last decade, including those who are successful in major scholarship competitions, have participated. I'm not surprised at the growing interest in undergraduate research as a national topic. I fully expect someday to see a national organization of similar stature to NAFA focused on undergraduate research, and the subject will surely become more prominent at our own meetings. To clear the way for even more of the same on our campus, we are also trying to refine a Freshman Research Program, which has significant recruiting appeal but, according to many of our faculty, is a contradiction in terms. As much as the one program delights me, the latter one frustrates, but I'm convinced the effort is worth it.

Of course, I could backtrack a little and say the most surprising development would be our seven-year run in Oxford and Cambridge with summer programs that seem to have remarkable effects on potential applicants. At the outset, one of our former students, a Rhodes Scholar, had generously offered to teach a literature course at Oxford for younger Scholar prospects, and we made that a reality with some help from alumni donors. This led us eventually to Cambridge where some of our best inter-disciplinary teachers designed courses that appealed to all disciplines—from agriculture to business to engineering, and everything in between. We knew we were on to something when out of one group of fifteen who attended, eleven eventually applied for major awards before graduating, and seven won—including two Gates winners in the same year. I mention this because it is an example of thinking creatively when an opportunity pops up that only needs a little attention and refinement. This year we are taking twenty to Cambridge for two weeks and Dublin for one week—a course on nineteenth century science and how related concepts show up in the works of James Joyce. Along those lines, we've tapped the NAFA rolls for special weekend courses here that have proven highly popular—one with long-time friend Tony Lisska from Dennison on natural philosophy, and just last year a great course with Bob Cochran from the University of Arkansas on plains history and culture, based on his memorable lecture at Denver on the same subject.

Why is it, then, that I sometimes feel concerned over the office and wonder if I'm still serving the students as effectively as in the past? Nearly twenty years is a long time at this pace, I'm not embarrassed to say. As I write I'm staring fearfully at the calendar, which shows me I have three to four weeks to advise seven Truman and Goldwater candidates as they finish their applications. Things are going very fast now, and I find myself obsessing over on-line applications and what might help, or hurt, my students' efforts. I think—"what lies between my wonderful students and possible fulfillment of a lifelong dream of a scholarship is a computer," something I know very little about but spend increasing amounts of time with. And when I'm not trying to figure out how to manage all that information, more new duties have come up that I have trouble fitting in—fund raising and recruiting chief among them. Three years ago my students banded together and purchased a new sofa for us, to commemorate all those sometimes harrowing and sometimes thrilling years in our office: going over essays, practicing interviews, and celebrating or comforting, depending. I do not see their successors as much anymore in "real time"—no need with attachments and uploads, not to mention a schedule of speeches and obligations that are supposed to serve a larger purpose of raising money and bringing in outstanding freshmen. But without "face time" (as opposed to "face-book time"), I fear little of the rest will work very well, and it sure will not be as much fun.

Is it possible things will change even faster in the next decade than they have since we first gathered in Fayetteville to learn how to "break the code"? Probably. I've now accepted how critical it is to maintain a thoroughly modern website for the students exploring our programs, and am taking steps to that end, with a wonderful graduate student's assistance. I read every message that NAFAns send through the listserv, and am still excited when new ideas pop up, or better yet, when a veteran rescues a new advisor with a quick tip or two. And I'm glad we're still sharing information and trying to imitate each other.

The first topic in those first days in 1999 that we knew had to be addressed was ethics. I have to think NAFA's first accomplishment, and why there are hundreds of members and schools now on our rolls, is easy to see. Yes, the organization let us meet and learn from others who knew how to make students more competitive, but more importantly we realized our true mission was to protect this important shared educational enterprise by combining our time and efforts with our collected conscience.

Oh yes—what about that *defining moment* I pondered last month after seeing my friends and colleagues, the reason I started writing this, the one I would pick that illustrates what we are trying to accomplish, in the final analysis. How about the following? Several years ago we had a student who won four major awards in two years—most amazing thing I have ever seen. He had one crucial and natural gift, I suppose one would say—in athletic terms, one that "could not be coached." That is, he was articulate and confident in the extreme under pressure, dominating an interview. During the same year, another brilliant and determined young man reached the final stages of three major awards, including two that the first person successfully completed. Unfortunately, his interviewing style was less effective; and in fact (to continue the athletic metaphor) he tended to "freeze" at "crunch time." Later, it was our fate one day, our pleasure and our agony, to have both of those young men in our office at once—celebrating and laughing in one room, and hugging and consoling next door—back and forth we went. You know the feeling.

What happened next made me think Scholar Development here was in pretty good shape because the head of a department, a very generous alumnus, and our office put our collective heads (and budgets) together and surprised our "runner-up" at graduation with nearly a full scholarship for Cambridge, where he received a master's in his dream program and has never looked back. Now that's what I call winning; no, better yet, in NAFA terminology and with a nod to a past conference, I'm happy to say that's "beyond winning."

5

Student Ambassadors in the Age of Anti-Americanism

CAROL MADISON GRAHAM

Carol Madison Graham holds advanced degrees from Georgetown University in Middle East History and International Relations. She began her involvement in international education as a U.S. diplomat. She moved to London in 1995 with her family where she has worked in the higher education, law, and government sectors. From 2002 to late 2006 she was Executive Director of the U.S. U.K. Fulbright Commission. During that time she founded the U.K. Scholarship Network for heads of U.K.-based scholarship organizations and was heavily involved in initiatives to increase diversity of institutions and students in scholarships on the United Kingdom European and international level. She is currently writing a guide to anti-Americanism for the U.S. study abroad community. Ms. Graham serves on a number of boards including the Carnegie U.K. Trust.

In 1942 the U.S. War Department saw fit to issue a small booklet to its personnel entitled "Instructions for American Servicemen in Britain 1942." Although the United States and Britain were allies and one might reasonably have expected the British to welcome the Americans, someone in the government wisely recognized that the soldiers (many of whom would be living overseas for the first time) would need guidance. The most impressive part of the book is the attempt to preserve the dignity of the British public from the slight regard of the soldiers coming from a more powerful country, physically untouched by the war and rationing. Detailed explanations touched on why the British were shabbily dressed, why their meals were not plentiful, and why there was potential for bad relations with British soldiers and families over the womenfolk. All of these issues and more are dealt with in an impressive manner that could put most international cultural briefings to shame.

Today, thousands of Americans are going overseas for the first time as foreign students, yet are they as well prepared as the solider in 1942? Most cultural briefings—if they even take place and the student attends them—will speak of euphoria, homesickness, culture shock, adjustment, and re-entry as though the student were going off in the space shuttle rather than to live in a foreign society. Deeming it impossible to deal with the entire world in a briefing for students setting off to different countries, many campuses with the capacity leave the specifics to in-country briefings. These briefings focus on the nitty gritty: courtesy, language, drinking and dating habits, transport, bank accounts, safety, and of course administration and program content. They may also provide the student with extracurricular events designed to increase appreciation for the host culture. All of this information is crucial and of intense interest to the student, and yet something is still missing.

Anti-Americanism has been present for decades in many parts of the world and has intensified due to recent events on the world stage. It has been written about and analyzed by experts who study it, but in many cases are not exposed to it on a daily basis so even if they were in the business of briefing students, they would not know what to say. You have to live overseas to fully understand what it consists of and why it happens. This is obviously difficult for U.S. college advisors, so in the world of upbeat and encouraging student briefings, anti-Americanism is the elephant in the room. We all know it is there, but few know how to deal with it. And deal with it we must because anti-American sentiment is something the student cannot glean from a textbook. Nor does experiencing it necessarily help the student to cope, understand it, or touch it as much of it is expressed in the media, leaving the student feeling frustrated.

For those who would argue that such sentiments are part of the student experience, and the best thing is to say nothing and let the student "figure it out," it is important to note that international experience can reinforce stereotypes and negative attitudes as well as eliminate them. Ask any European. The danger of not explaining anti-Americanism properly and arming the student with coping strategies can lead to conclusions damaging to the student's understanding of and contact with the host country. Pinning negative comments on jealousy of the United States and lost empire complexes—certainly elements, but not the whole formula—distances students from the host society thereby reducing the possibility of not only learning, but also imparting information. In short, students' ability to fulfill the ambassadorial role they understand as part of their study abroad year is diminished. This is an important moment for the advisor to both serve the student and the public good.

The advising community has an opportunity to take the lead in moving student preparation and orientation forward. For those without overseas campuses and personnel, this can easily be done before departure because unfortunately anti-Americanism is a global phenomenon although local permutations obviously exist. Advisors do what they do because they care about students. Therefore seizing the initiative on this issue is important in the mission to assist students because today's U.S. citizen abroad is under ever more pressure and scrutiny. Moreover, failure to prepare the student may lead not to an overseas experience, but to an American experience transplanted overseas as the student decides to retreat into an American bubble without understanding how the environment has affected that decision. Not only are U.S. students coming under more pressure each year, but they also bear a lonely kind of burden that is not carried by their fellow foreign students. Relatively few people outside of Latin America understand the foreign policy of Brazil, nor do they know very much about Brazilian culture, so the Brazilian student may confront stereotypes about Brazil, but she will not find herself in the shadow of the harsh spotlight that is trained 24/7 on the United States and its citizens. It is vital to note that attention is not merely paid to the foreign policy of the United States, but also to the foreign policy of such companies as McDonald's.

What then is anti-Americanism for the U.S. student or permanent expat? What makes it different from the foreign policy, anti-Bush/anti-Americanism described by academics and journalists? Day-to-day anti-Americanism has to do not only with U.S. actions, but also with assumptions about the kind of society and people that produce those actions. Student exchange is about cultural curiosity and understanding—at least that is what we tell students. So the average American student alights in the foreign country ignorant (perhaps too much so) about the host country and eager to learn about the society, expecting that others will be just as curious. But the reality is that the student may not be the object of curiosity at all. In countries like Britain, there are so many resident Americans and U.S. tourists that the student may hardly be noticed in the major universities. This is particularly true of scholarship students who are often clustered in the same prestigious universities such as Oxford and Cambridge. Whether they are in the United Kingdom or somewhere with far fewer Americans, large swathes of U.S. culture are not considered to be foreign at all. The fact is, much of the world believes it already knows the United States so our students risk not being seen as individuals, but rather as part of a culture that has already been judged—judged and found wanting.

Among the British students I have interviewed, the image of the United States is that of a country of environmentally unfriendly policies (both private and public sector) bent on dominating the world through projection of military power. Even those who do not subscribe to this view of the United States agree to the prevalence of this picture. This representation exists among older people as well and includes other dislikes. Principal among these are the "Hollywood movies," a term that has come to mean formulaic films that clog the cinemas, crowding out other native films. The United States is seen as a place where religious fanatics thrive and unqualified Hollywood actors hold high political office, as a place where the general population has no interest or knowledge in world affairs yet exerts disproportionate influence on it, as a place where "unnecessary lawsuits" dominate the legal system, cultural integration is a myth, and democracy has gone too far (in the form of elected judges). Finally, and crucially for scholars of Marshall and other WWII-origin scholarships, the British resent what they regard as too much self-congratulation over the Second World War. As the U.S. government author of the instructions for 1942 servicemen pointed out, the British had held out alone against Hitler before the Americans entered the war. But for their tenacity in the face of the destruction of their major cities, the outcome of the war might have been quite different.

This is very heavy cultural baggage for a student, who may never have lived outside of the United States, to cart around Paris or London. Those who try and comfort students by telling them that they need not worry about anti-Americanism because it is only aimed at U.S. foreign policy decisions (as happened at an overseas briefing for scholarships students last year) are in fact missing the point in the context of student exchange. The student buys into this and believes that he/she only has to disagree publicly with the policy (or retreat from policy discussions if in agreement) and all will be well.[1] But Americans who live overseas know a different reality because day-to-day anti-Americanism is a view of American society. Far from being a new phenomenon, anti-Americanism has been present for years rumbling along like a dormant volcano. The role of foreign policy issues such as the war in Iraq is as a catalyst for eruption, but everyone knew the volcano was active before the lava came thundering down the mountainside. Besides, in Britain, it is perfectly clear to everyone that the British attacks on Bush and the war in Iraq are often motivated by a desire to get at the current Prime Minister. The British are sensitive to any situation in which they are treated as less than a full partner by the United States. Much of the country felt dragged into the war, but it is their own government they are blaming. By attacking the United States and Bush, they can get at Tony Blair in two ways, directly and indirectly. This is why those of us who live (and vote) overseas in local communities are less bothered by the foreign policy style anti-Americanism. We are far more aware of the general negative headlines, remarks, and commentaries, which have increased enormously.

Thus Americans overseas are used to holding their breath when their parish priest says "there is a joke about an American, a German and. . . ." We are also used to being told by newspapers and in our local gym that "whatever happens in the United States comes here." Sometimes these ideas and trends are positive, but over the years, Americans living abroad have noticed that this phrase refers to more and more unwelcome phenomena. I once remarked to a British colleague that to be American in Britain is to be told that everything is 900 years older than America, but that neither crime nor drugs existed in Britain until they were imported from the United States.

The image of the United States can also be tarnished by what does *not* appear in the media. After the tsunami in 2004, news in the print press reported that the United States was trying to help its tarnished world image by a massive operation. But I had to hear from American friends that the operation had been successful. There was plenty of TV coverage along the lines of "help is now coming to these people to rebuild their broken lives . . ." but not one U.S. ship was pictured. Eventually, I saw a tiny article on a news sidebar noting a BBC reporter's complaint that British television had not shown footage of the very effective U.S. effort. The reporter laid the oversight at the door of anti-Americanism. It made me think back to an incident that occurred years ago when I was a press officer at the U.S. Embassy in Beirut during the war. Most of my colleagues and I had been evacuated to Cyprus, where we became effectively seconded to the U.S. Embassy in Cyprus to assist with the citizen evacuation that had just been ordered (by the United States, Japan, Australia, and the European embassies). I was assigned to assist the U.S. embassy press counselor. A few hours after the evacuation began, I received a furious call from the embassy admin officer. The BBC was reporting scenes of confusion at the arrival site of the British and U.S. evacuation sites. I had missed this first report because I was at the scene talking to the evacuated U.S. reporters. He was certainly right to be upset. The operation was impeccably organized. When the evacuees arrived they found their bags neatly laid out in rows, with plenty of marines and officials (I was one of them) to assist. I called the BBC reporter, whom I knew well. He was normally stationed in Beirut but like me was now in Cyprus working. He was mortified that his story had been edited so badly and apologized profusely. He had apparently noted that there were scenes of confusion at the *British* evacuation site only and had indeed seen for himself that the evacuees at our site were surprised and impressed that everything was so well planned. He protested to the head office in London and tried to have the story (which repeated every few minutes) changed but they refused. At the time I put this down to a reputable news organization not wanting to admit it had been wrong in the slightest detail. But years later, living in Britain, I sometimes wonder if this was not my first glimpse of the "we don't want to praise Americans!" attitude with which I was so wearily familiar in the Middle East.

For the record, I find that British journalists reporting on the United States are outstanding. Their reporting is fair, incisive, and thorough—once they come to grips with the multiple power centers and get out of Washington and New York, which they all seem to do eventually. It was instructive that a U.K. Fulbright alumna and journalist told me she had tried to get assigned to the United States or to report on U.S. issues but was refused on the grounds that she was "biased" since she had been living in the United States. I wonder if they would have made the same decision is she had been studying in Latin America or Japan and wanted to cover them? Her anecdote indicated to me that among those with no in-depth U.S. experience we are not seen as a society with a real history or culture that might require an expert. They clearly had interpreted her enthusiasm and affection for the United States as somehow impairing her abilities as a journalist—as if she had been subjected to minor brainwashing techniques. And those of us used to derogatory stories in the press would add that perhaps they were certainly concerned lest some of her reports paint the United States in a positive light.

Americans abroad notice frequent instances of the "we don't praise the United States" phenomenon. A striking example was the introduction of citizenship tests and ceremonies in the United Kingdom. Until recently new citizens in the United Kingdom applied for citizenship, swore an oath before a lawyer in an office, signed a form, then sent it back, and eventually received a certificate. It was an administrative procedure. No test. No official oath taking. No welcome speech. When they decided to introduce citizenship tests and ceremonies, officials were quoted as *reassuring* the public that they were not going to introduce "U.S. style" ceremonies, which were criticized as being too much like a party (it was implied that these were vulgar displays of patriotism). Officials embarked on a series of fact-finding trips to a number of countries including, we were told, Canada, but the United States appears to have been studiously avoided. So the one thing the United States does well and in which we truly have experience—making new citizens welcome—was deemed not worthy of attention due to the government's knowledge of generalized anti-American sentiment among the public, which may have been shared by particular officials.

What then are the sources of anti-Americanism overseas and especially in the United Kingdom, our closest ally? In my opinion, there are three. The first is the same as the source of culture shock: the presence of the two cultures living side by side. In a culture shock situation, the two cultures reside in the student and in the student's environment, so the student feels internal pressure. In the case of anti-Americanism, United States culture is living side by side with British culture in the cinema, in cyberspace, in shopping malls, and in the vocabulary being adopted by the young. In both cases the two cultures act like tectonic plates rubbing up against each other. If there is too much friction, a natural disaster ensues. In other words, a certain amount of anti-Americanism is slightly xenophobic and can be compared with other feelings harbored against other foreign cultures in all countries.

Second, there is the issue of cultural "slighting." *Slighting* is a term used for castles and fortresses. When a castle was to be a place that might well harbor opposition, the King ordered the castle to be "slighted" or rendered indefensible by putting a hole in the main wall or particular towers. Slighting did not involve destroying the entire castle—just strategic parts of it. In this way, the castle became picturesque and historic, but lost its purpose and usefulness except ultimately as a tourist attraction.

The British and many others around the world feel that their cultures are being slighted. That their whole being has been usurped and consigned to a tourist attraction by Americans whose own culture, thanks to superpower status, appears omnipresent. It is important to note that while everyone is proud of his history, no one wants to believe his own culture and institutions have no future. We all want to be acknowledged for the contribution we are making today as well as the contributions of our ancestors. This largely unarticulated feeling is a powerful source of anti-Americanism. So telling inhabitants of Oxford how "historic" their town is may be received politely, but could have the opposite effect intended and be perceived as lack of respect.

Third, and most importantly, much anti-Americanism is due to a profound lack of knowledge of U.S. history and culture, an ignorance made all the more tragic and difficult to contend with, given that other countries are awash with images and information in snippets about contemporary America. Non-Americans are in possession of a lot of knowledge—perhaps too much about the United States—but it is the wrong kind of knowledge for our purposes because it takes small slices of life as the whole and only talks about the present.

This creates a curious paradox that I used to put to British Fulbright students going to the United States. Americans think the British live in the past and the British think Americans do not have one. This is a structural problem based in our school (not college) curricula. Americans obviously have to study some European history as a prelude to the explorers and conquistadors. We consider British history part of American history. Similarly our high school English classes include English literature. However, the inclusion of Britain in history books is necessarily intermittent and often stops after WWII. Most Americans have some knowledge of British history and literature, but not much knowledge of modern Britain. The British on the other hand, having a great deal of ground to cover, place very little if any American history and little or no U.S. literature on the high school syllabus, but they know a lot about contemporary American society thanks to the media. This same situation can be multiplied across the world. The United States is *the* modern country for millions of non-Americans especially, although not exclusively, for young people. The idea that we have historical roots can even be threatening to their image of the United States as the place where the future begins—just as threatening as the idea is to us that the British and others are not the rigid traditional societies we would sometimes like them to be.

After thirty years of living overseas and explaining the United States to non-Americans, I have concluded that this view that we have no history is the key ingredient of anti-Americanism because it informs a general stance toward the United States. Many Europeans have said to me "of course to us the United States has no history." For many years I accepted it as an irritating party joke but in the course of the discussion on particular topics (religion, race relations, the South) I was forced to conclude that there was more truth in it than I or they thought at the time. The American Revolution is known; therefore they obviously acknowledge that we have a past. But this is not the same thing as accepting that the United States has a history. That is, they allow that events have occurred since and indeed before 1776, but they do not understand how these events had a coherence that inform our actions. Nor do they possess the detail that explains why these actions occurred and made sense to the actors. In other words, to them it is not a history but instead a series of dates. There is obviously no blame to be attached in this. Nevertheless, the American student overseas may suffer for this lack of knowledge.

For example, a student may be confronted with quite virulent attacks on U.S. foreign policy with the addition that the United States does not know what it is doing. An oft repeated accusation is that the United States has no real experience in foreign affairs since it "has no real history." I have been hearing this for twenty years in many countries. As it happens, we have a great deal of experience in foreign affairs, but it does not follow that experience always creates successful policies. Every country in the world can look to its own history for the truth of it. To say that we have an incorrect or failed policy is to attack our policy—fair enough. To say that we have an incorrect policy because we are too inexperienced is to attack our culture as an immature culture.

Finally, there is an element that fuels anti-Americanism in a similar way as the foreign policy issues: the well-publicized ignorance of Americans in world geography and in foreign affairs generally.[2] The National Council for Geographic Education points out on its website that this lack of knowledge is "a threat to our nation's security" and also an "embarrassment." It *is* an embarrassment and the opprobrium has seeped right down to the local British schools. (I am extremely lucky that the British school attended by my children is sensitive to other cultures. Questions about the United States appear on general knowledge quizzes and the *Star Spangled Banner* is played on the 4th of July. This is done out of goodwill and the desire to make life interesting and fun for the children since to my knowledge the only American children at the school are mine. An American friend of mine has had the opposite experience. Her son's primary school produced an end of year newsletter with an article highlighting and commenting on the lack of geographical knowledge by U.S. students. The article was called "American Idiots." Another article criticized George Bush and had a drawing of him wearing what resembled red devil ears. No other country, including Britain, was featured. Only the United States was fair game. The article was written, it turns out, by two parents. Her protest to the school pointed out that the newspaper was meant to raise money for and be distributed among veterans, who would have fought side by side with Americans. The response from the school was polite incomprehension. The principal was "sorry that she had taken offense . . ." My friend later found that her son had been subjected to anti-American comments by one of his teachers for years.)

This particular survey has been in the press for some time and is repeated from time to time. It is interesting that surveys on science knowledge or languages are not publicized in Britain. Venturing a guess, there are probably two reasons for this. The first is that British students might fare as badly as or worse than Americans. The second is that geographical and world knowledge are deemed by most people, and certainly by those from countries that commanded extensive empires, to be most pertinent for the citizens of a world power. That the United States can command such influence in the world, and yet have citizens whose world knowledge is so restricted, is not only incredible in their view, but also frightening. Their fear and frustration then is converted into or fuels hostility of the United States—especially when the United States pursues policies that are unpopular. As if the fact that a twelve-year-old does not know where river Volga is located was responsible for the United States refusing to sign the Kyoto accords.

This is not to defend the ignorance of Americans in this or any other domain, quite the contrary. But merely to point out that the surveys are also of concern in the United States and that they reflect a serious gap in the U.S. education system, not the fact that Americans are idiots or that the agencies running foreign policy do not know anything about the world. At the same time this is precisely why scholarship students going abroad are so valuable to the United States. They have tremendous potential to balance the views of the United States in local communities but only if they too are prepared—especially before they depart.

What can they and their advisors do? First of all, update the meaning of the word *ambassador*. Sending the student as an ambassador is too often interpreted as projecting an image: being courteous, continuing to study well, and exuding friendliness. In short, just following the behavior that got them the scholarship in the first place. Minority students sometimes take the definition further by believing that their presence in a particular country will show that Americans are diverse. However the U.S. media has been of tremendous assistance in changing the multicultural expectations of much of the world and certainly in Europe. Europeans know full well if they have gone anywhere near an American movie or TV show that the United States has African Americans, Asian Americans, Muslims, Jewish people, and so on. And even if the student manages to astonish the host country nationals with his/her background what then? The student is now considered an American and will also be subject to the anti-American comments like everyone else.

Given the sources of anti-Americanism, today's students need to understand the *United States* much better. If they have not had much contact with the minority or the majority, whatever that may mean in their context, they should do some reading and start networking. Like real diplomats, the object is not so much to defend the United States in conversation as to explain it. Nine times out of ten, comments are made because the United States is misunderstood. After a simple or sometimes not-so-simple explanation the attitude changes completely and a real dialogue begins with benefits on both sides but particularly for the student. Ignorance of basic facts about the United States should never be underestimated. A taxi driver nearly had an accident when I told him that the United States had publicly funded hospitals and that communities voted on whether they wished to pay for additional services. Many governments are far more centralized than the United States. In Britain, local communities, so treasured by us all, have no real say over hospital and other services. Britain has no local income tax. This is not to say our system is better—something students including scholarship students are guilty of concluding in public from time to time. On the other hand, just because we do not have a National Health Service it does not follow that only wealthy Americans have access to doctors.

Students should begin with refamiliarizing themselves with the Constitution and even the Federalist Papers as the ethos of the United States is different from that of non-revolution countries (or those like Britain where the revolution did not involve starting from a blank slate). The fact that the Constitution is still the law of the land is news indeed to others and our approach to freedom of speech and religion (both frequently criticized as excessive) will be valuable tools in explaining the United States.

The second action students must take—if they really wish to be effective in their role as an ambassador—is meet the host nationals, who are not themselves college or graduate students. These days this is easier said than done, especially for scholarship students who are very busy and sometimes also very isolated in centers of excellence with other foreigners or a slice of the population that is unimpressed with being in the classroom with Americans. Volunteering in the community—even if it is done just once— is the most fun and rewarding way to engage with people. Regular attendance at a religious institution: a church, synagogue, temple, or mosque is a wonderful way to meet people of all ages who may not be used to U.S.

students. It is also a great way to find volunteer activities. In Western Europe, churches in particular are short-handed. Through the religious institutions and sometimes through the universities themselves, students who would like to speak to school children will find contacts or perhaps programs already in place. However, keeping in mind the media environment, the information must be new and interesting to the students. This is where extensive knowledge of the United States on a foreign affairs subject like climate change is necessary. Scholarship students expecting an enthusiastic response to their research or a simplistic view of what life is like in the United States may be disappointed. In order to be effective they have to know much more about the United States than the students they are meeting.

Studying abroad is an exciting experience, but it is also a far braver venture into another society than students may know at the outset. For those who truly engage with the society, meeting anti-American sentiment is inevitable. An encounter with it can be depressing, distressing, and demoralizing but it is also a tremendous opportunity to fulfill their ambassador role in a way that truly has impact. If their experience is anything like my study abroad year in Turkey, they will also gain valuable training in reacting with calm and thinking on their feet—skills that are essential in the high pressure careers for which many are headed. Instead of ignoring anti-Americanism, students need to prepare for it. In this way they will both gain and impart cultural insights so often missing in international exchanges.

6

Alternative Winning

JANE MORRIS

Jane Morris is a 1978 graduate of Villanova University with both a B.S. in Biology and a B.A. in Honors. After receiving an M.A. in Biology from Bryn Mawr College, Jane worked as a research scientist in both the private and public sector for nearly twenty years. In September 2001, she became Villanova's first director of Competitive Grants and Awards. In this capacity, Ms. Morris provides guidance for students applying for nationally competitive scholarships and direction for the Connelly Delouvrier International Scholars Program, the Presidential Scholarship Program, and the Villanova University Undergraduate Student Collaborative Research Awards. In addition, Ms. Morris currently serves as secretary for NAFA. In 2004 and 2006, she directed site visits by NAFA members to universities in the United Kingdom, Ireland, and Northern Ireland.

There are thirty-two American Rhodes Scholars elected every year, forty to forty-four Marshall Scholars, twelve Mitchell Scholars, thirty to thirty-five Gates Cambridge Scholars, and seventy-five Truman Scholars. Applying for these highly prestigious awards are nearly 3,500 candidates, most of whom have been through a campus screening process. There is approximately a five to six percent chance of winning and a ninety-four to ninety-five percent chance of losing. These are staggering odds. As scholarship advisors, we understand that not everyone will win a nationally competitive scholarship, but we believe fervently that the process of applying for these awards has a value for our students, beyond winning.

The value of the process—sometimes I hear these words and I want to scream. Usually this occurs after what feels like hundreds of hours of working with scholarship applicants as they prepare their program statements and personal statements, secure letters of recommendation, interview with campus selection committees, all while maintaining their near-perfect grade point averages and service commitments. This is a grueling and often painful process which, according to the previous statistics, more often than not, yields a negative outcome. It is hard to remember the "value of the process" when an unsuccessful candidate sits in the office sobbing. Believe me, the last thing that student wants to hear in that moment is "the value of the process."

Once the sobbing subsides, however, the real rewards from having pursued such a worthwhile goal eventually begin to appear in the lives of these students as they gain acceptance to and often funding for highly competitive graduate programs, law schools, medical schools, and public service positions around the world. Moreover, they have been through a process of serious self-reflection at a critical juncture in their lives, opening themselves up to the scrutiny of strangers. What they learn from these exercises has value beyond measure. They learn to look at themselves as potential Rhodes Scholars or Marshall Scholars, to assimilate all they have learned through academics with their experiences of the world through their service to the community, both at home and internationally. They begin to see themselves as future leaders and agents of global change. One might call this "alternative winning."

Since coming to Villanova as the director of Undergraduate Grants and Awards in the fall of 2001, I have had the honor of guiding the preparation of nearly 300 applications for nationally competitive scholarships. Each of the candidates with whom I have worked has been exceptionally well-qualified. Notable among these students were the members of the class of 2004. Perhaps it was because I met them as sophomores in the wake of September 11, but each one I met seemed more amazing than the next. Five of these students were finalists in the 2003–2004 Rhodes competition, one was a Gates Cambridge finalist and five advanced in the Fulbright. While four were awarded grants through Fulbright, none came home with the Rhodes or the Gates Cambridge. Every member of this cohort has gone on to post-graduate studies, most with funding. Many have now finished at least a master's degree and some have gone on to Ph.D. programs or law school. Others are venturing out to work in NGOs in third-world nations or are preparing to enter multinational corporations. One has started his own non-profit organization to inspire civic engagement among America's youth. As an illustration of the wonders of alternative winning, I offer you the stories of five members of the class of 2004.

One day in April of 2002, a whirlwind blew into my office. Armed with a charismatic energy that illuminated my tiny office on the fourth floor, Ryan came with a mission—he wanted to learn how the scholarship application process could prepare him to eradicate mediocrity and apathy among American youth. Ryan was majoring in political science with an eye toward running for public office one day. His charm was bound very tightly with intelligence and humility that no doubt came from being the eldest of six children born into a working class family from Carson City, Nevada. Coming to Villanova was both courageous and difficult for this young man whose swimming prowess helped support his attendance at Villanova. He understood the value in working hard and in embracing new challenges.

Over the course of the next couple of years as Ryan began the process of scholarship application, I learned that Ryan's work ethic was coupled with a keen mental focus and attention to detail. Ryan attributed this discipline to the training he received from his high school swimming coach, a former Chinese Olympic swimmer. In fact, the lessons he learned from his coach led Ryan to his lifelong passion for China. He attended Chinese kindergarten as a fourteen-year-old and completed a minor in Chinese language at Villanova. Ryan believed that in order to become a political leader in the United States, having a strong appreciation for other cultures—especially the growing global importance of China—was critical. In his senior year, Ryan took advantage of every opportunity he could to advance his knowledge of China: applying for a Fulbright to China, a Rhodes and Marshall to study International Relations at Oxford, and a Gates Cambridge to pursue an MPhil in Chinese Studies. We were all excited when Ryan was selected as a Nevada State finalist for the Rhodes. Sadly, Ryan didn't advance. Ryan was more successful in the Fulbright competition. Selected first as an alternate, Ryan had to decline the grant when he finally received it because he had been accepted to a program at Cambridge which included an eight-month stay in China that complemented his studies of Chinese economics.

During his time in China, Ryan conducted a research project on political participation in China. In addition, he used his expanding competence in Mandarin and his experience as a swimmer to facilitate business deals between Chinese and American sporting goods companies in anticipation of the Beijing Olympics in 2008. Throughout the course of his experiences in China, Ryan provided stunning narratives of his visits to Chinese villages and his many excursions to the Great Wall. I often felt as though I were right there with him at table with a Chinese family or camping out under the stars on the Great Wall. At Cambridge, Ryan performed extremely well earning mostly distinctions on his exams and this past spring, he was a finalist for the White House Fellowship.

How does Ryan feel about the value of the scholarship application process? Here are his words:

> *Applying for the various scholarships was a process that forced me to find my core. I had to dig very deep to hone in on those key values and beliefs that shape every action I take and every decision I ponder. Discovering that core during my senior year was invaluable, as I was able to capitalize on many opportunities when I left the safety of Villanova and began my adventure to the outside world of Cambridge and then China. I also was able to form close friendships with some other stellar Villanovans applying for similar opportunities, and keeping in touch with them over the past few years and learning about their various experiences broadened my perspective as well.*

> *I will graduate from the University of Cambridge in October, having received mostly distinctions on my exams. . . . I am pursuing various opportunities with international financial institutions including Goldman Sachs, HSBC, and some hedge funds. I am looking to apply my Mandarin skills and expand my knowledge of the economic relationship between the United States and China. Apart from my career, I am also heading up a non-profit organization called Youth Voice, Inc. Inspired by Alexis De Tocqueville's Democracy in America, it is one of America's first non-profit organizations run solely by people under twenty-six years old geared at fostering a new sense of civic involvement among America's youth through education, motivation, and participation.*

Ryan is a winner.

When Bruce was a young boy growing up in the suburbs of St. Louis, he and his family would pack up the family station wagon and head to Bush Stadium to see the Cardinals play. On one notable, very hot day, Bruce witnessed homelessness for the first time as they passed a family sitting outside on their mattress "home" on the way to the game. Even as a nine-year-old, Bruce could not help but question the circumstances that allowed his garage-parked car to have better protection from the elements than this couple and their two small children. Fifteen years later, Bruce continues to ask this same question.

As a student at Villanova, Bruce directed his studies toward an intellectual and experiential understanding of the underlying social causes for poverty and homelessness. Internships with organizations such as Housing Comes First and Philadelphia Committee to End Homelessness as well as volunteering for a Philadelphia-based after-school program exposed Bruce to the realities of poverty in our community. On mission trips to Costa Rica and Mexico, he expanded his worldview by working with development agencies on projects involving cultural immersion and development of urban infrastructure. Not content to relegate his experiences to extracurricular activities, Bruce coupled his volunteering with academic research, presenting his first paper, *The Racialization of Welfare: Perceptions of Inequality Creating the Racial Cleavage in Welfare Support,* as a freshman. Bruce's Truman Policy Proposal on the reform of Section 8 Housing as well as his commitment to activism earned Bruce an interview for the Truman in his junior year. He didn't win, but he continued to pursue nationally competitive scholarships in his senior year. Bruce was a state finalist for the Rhodes Scholarship and an alternate for a Fulbright to Hungary to study homelessness in post-Communist cities. After Villanova, Bruce worked for the NYC Economic Development Corporation as a New York Urban Fellow while he applied again for the Marshall to attend the London School of Economics (LSE) where he had been accepted to study for an MSc in City, Space, and Society in the Department of Human Geography. When for the second time the Marshall eluded him, Bruce opted to take out loans to attend LSE, and he has now completed his master's studies and will be starting a Ph.D. in Cultural and Social Anthropology at Stanford University in the fall. At Stanford, Bruce's research will focus on the relationship between governance and the built form (buildings, boulevards, and public transportation, for example) in post-Communist cities. In June of 2007,

Bruce will begin research as a Fulbright Scholar in this area in Bucharest, Romania. Bruce has been tenacious in seeking the opportunities that will position him to become a credible authority on the subject of homelessness and the ways to restructure the institutions that allow poverty to flourish. About his experience with the scholarship process, Bruce commented,

> *Applying for nationally competitive scholarships was one of the best decisions that I made as an undergraduate. Even if one falls short of "winning," the process of researching, drafting and networking that any of the national fellowships entails leaves one well positioned for graduate school applications. In the case of the Fulbright, the initial attempt provided a helpful starting point and a wealth of experience that made my second go around much more successful.*

Bruce is a winner.

Krista was an English major with a deeply rooted social conscience formed from a love of reading tightly linked to an inherent sense of fairness. She was led to my office by the hand of her history professor who insisted that she embark upon the scholarship application process as a way to channel her energies and find direction for her abiding need to rectify systemic injustices. To my delight, Krista was a frequent visitor to my office as she worked to discern how she would address these issues. I would find myself looking forward to our conversations because they could range from discussions of the moral complexities in *Crime and Punishment,* to last week's episode of *The West Wing,* to presidential election politics, or to her varied experiences with the Appalachian Service Project. Krista was a voracious reader and uncompromising student who had strong, well-founded opinions about many important issues. One of these issues was poverty and its eradication. In her Truman scholarship application, Krista wrote passionately about her anger with poverty and the network of devastating consequences for individuals as well as institutions. She was a finalist in this competition but unfortunately, did not receive the scholarship. In her senior year, Krista applied for both the Marshall and the Rhodes (she was selected as a state finalist). While disappointed to again come home without the prize, Krista was nonetheless edified by the experience:

> *The scholarship process forced me to think bigger than I had been thinking previously. Having professors tell me I should be applying for some of these prestigious awards was both surprising and flattering; the process actually*

altered the scale of my goals. The experience gave me the opportunity to interact with and compare plans with both my own classmates at Villanova and also with the other Truman and Rhodes interviewees, and their ambitions and accomplishments also gave me a higher standard of what to measure myself against than simply getting good grades at Nova. It made—and still makes—a difference just to feel that I am in their league and similarly capable of making a mark on the world.

Also, the process forced me to really think critically about what I was hoping to do with my life after college, in a way I otherwise may have put off for years. It was in trying to determine where and what I wanted to study while applying for the Truman that I first let a professor talk to me about policy being a "proactive" way to address the issues I cared about. I don't know that I ever would have thought of policy on my own, but the idea took hold and the more I wrote to convince others that this was a good path for me, the more I believed it myself. As I'm about to start my first "real" job after grad school, I can't claim that I'm sure I'll be doing this the rest of my life, but I do know that it feels like a natural fit for me, and I am looking forward to jumping in. (And if I change my mind in a few years, the scholarship process and my entire Villanova experience also convinced me I have the potential to do whatever else I set my mind to. . . .)

After graduating *summa cum laude* from Villanova, Krista received a full-tuition graduate fellowship to pursue a master's in public policy at George Washington University, concentrating in social policy. While at George Washington, Krista did part-time policy work for a non-profit affordable housing organization, the National Housing Trust. Last spring, Krista was a finalist for the Presidential Management Fellows Program. She will soon be starting a new position with the National Institutes of Health doing program evaluation.

Krista is a winner.

When I think of Caitlin, the word "incandescent" comes to mind. She is, simply, lit from within. In a letter of recommendation, one of Caitlin's professors wrote, "The affective dimension of her life is inextricably tied to her ability to locate the presence of beauty in each of her intellectual endeavors. If the human soul has a special language for experiential integrity, Caitlin has come as close to mastering it as anyone whom I have come to know." I can't think of a better way to describe this capable and committed young woman. Caitlin was among the first students I met when I started my job at Villanova. My colleague introduced me to a group of young men and women getting ready for their weekly trek to North Philadelphia to tutor middle school students. I was struck by the energy of the group, but moved when one young woman graciously came forward, introduced herself to me, and immediately welcomed me warmly into the honors program family. That was Caitlin. Since then, I have come to know Caitlin as so much more than a bright, enthusiastic sophomore serving the underprivileged. She has matured into a woman committed to eradicating the causes of injustice, poverty, and oppression—a woman committed intellectually and spiritually to the principles of radical love.

A self-avowed lover of words, Caitlin's fascination with language led her toward a major in Spanish with a minor in Latin American studies. A service trip to Guatemala in her freshman year at Villanova awakened Caitlin to the realities of poverty in the developing world and to an understanding of the transformative power of language. Once ignited, Caitlin's need to understand the powerful tension between poverty and privilege was insatiable. She spent a semester in Costa Rica working on human rights issues among migrant workers in the banana zone. Once again, Caitlin's affinity for language opened her to immersing herself to life in Costa Rica, where she developed both a rural Costa Rican accent and a profound solidarity with the poor.

All of these experiences led Caitlin to apply for nationally competitive scholarships when she returned to campus in her senior year. Intent on one day returning to Costa Rica, Caitlin took advantage of every opportunity to learn more about Latin America and the issues facing migrant groups there. In addition to applying for a Fulbright to study at the International Center for Sustainable Human Development (CIDH) in Costa Rica, Caitlin applied to pursue Latin American studies through the Rhodes, the Marshall, and the Gates Cambridge. Getting an interview for the Gates Cambridge was very exciting, and we were all very hopeful for Caitlin. Frustrated with an unpleasant interview experience with the Gates, Caitlin was happy when she learned that she was awarded a Fulbright to complete a research project on transculturation of Nicaraguans in Costa Rica. During her Fulbright year, Caitlin reapplied for a Gates Cambridge scholarship and was again disappointed. After her year in Costa Rica, Caitlin decided to attend Cambridge to read for an M.Phil. in Latin American studies with financial support through Cambridge Trusts. Caitlin excelled in her studies there and has now returned to Costa Rica to continue her work with CIDH. Caitlin's future plans include Ph.D. studies, but for now, she is excited about being back in Costa Rica.

Looking back on the scholarship application process with all of the ups and the downs, Caitlin reflects,

> I think the most important parts of the whole scholarship process senior (and junior) year were that without them, I would never have thought of living outside the country. I really wanted to go back to Costa Rica after study abroad, but I didn't know how I could do that, and suddenly you appeared and said the magic word—Fulbright! Writing those personal statements and project proposals helped me to focus all of my ideas about what I wanted to do after Villanova. Also, on a more personal level, I really liked working with everyone on the scholarships—I never felt like we were competing; it was neat to help proofread Nate's essays, to share with peers the experience of trying to explain yourself on paper in less than 500 words. Trying to hone in on recommendation writers also made me realize how much I enjoyed working with my various professors and that they too appreciated me.

> And you know, while I wanted to return to Costa Rica, I would never have thought of studying in England. And now that the degree is done, and (even though it was a very difficult year, I learned SOOOO much) I had so many amazing opportunities to bask in a super academic environment, and learn so much about new disciplines as well as about myself.

Caitlin is a winner.

Nate's story illustrates the finest qualities of the Class of 2004. Nate, Krista, and Caitlin were among a select group of students in the Honors Program who completed Interdisciplinary Humanities, an intense sequence of classes in their freshman and sophomore years. There is a special, lasting bond that forms among the students in these courses, forged through the rigors of the academics and sustained through the knowledge that they not only survived, they thrived. In the fall of 2003, this community came together to help Nate in a way that is indelibly etched in my memory.

Nate is a phenomenon. I first met him at the annual reception for Villanova's Presidential Scholars where he stood out (quite literally at 6' 4") for both his grace and his graciousness. I soon learned that practically everyone on campus knew Nate—he was involved in a plethora of activities from *a capella* singing, to Residence Life, to club volleyball. An Eagle Scout from a very close-knit family in Pittsburgh, Nate had a profound respect for nature and the environment which resulted in an Environmental studies concentration in addition to his majors in communications and Honors. Having grown up in Pittsburgh, Nate was witness to the urban rebirth of this former iron and steel manufacturing city. Nate's love for his city and his commitment to the environment sparked in him an interest in urban development utilizing green design. His curiosity led him to an internship with the Regional Industrial Development Corporation in Pittsburgh and became the topic of his senior thesis. When Nate returned to school in his senior year, he was determined to continue his studies of urban development and was intrigued by the idea of doing so in England. All of his life, his grandmother kept telling him he should apply for a Rhodes Scholarship and so the dutiful grandson did just that, applying to study for an M.Sc. in Environmental Change and Management. Nate also applied for a Marshall Scholarship.

Three days before the deadline for Rhodes, Nate learned that his uncle and godfather, whom he adored, had passed away after a long battle with cancer. While Nate had finished his essay, the application wasn't quite ready and so his Interdisciplinary Humanities colleagues—some of whom were fellow scholarship applicants—rallied around him to help him finish so he could go home for the funeral. While a couple of students ran through a final proofread of his essay and resume, another loving friend sat with Nate at the typewriter filling in Page A-5, and another group copied and collated. As I stood in the office witnessing all of this activity, I couldn't help but wonder what powerful forces love and friendship are. Nate's application was the first one to go out.

Nate wasn't selected as a finalist for either the Rhodes or the Marshall. While I know he was a little disappointed by this, he nevertheless continued to pursue avenues that would lead him to his goal. He applied for and received a Coro Fellowship in Public Affairs in his beloved Pittsburgh. The Coro experience was incredible. Recently, Nate sent me a narrative about his fellowship year and the plans he has for his future.

As the end of my time at Villanova drew closer, I started investigating postgraduate options with "out of the ordinary" experiences in mind. Knowing I wanted to focus on urban redevelopment and environmental issues, I applied for fellowships with unique learning opportunities in lands far away—Oxford, Spain, Ireland. Jane Morris, however, knowing my hometown love for Pittsburgh, Pennsylvania, suggested that I also look into the Coro Fellowship Program in Public Affairs. With a recently opened program in the home in the 'burgh, I applied thinking it would be a good option. What transpired over the subsequent year shocked and invigorated me while introducing me to much more of myself and the city I love than I ever imagined possible.

Coro is a national program based in seven cities across the country dedicated to preparing young professionals to work in multifaceted public policy arenas. The secondary goal is to create a network of support that encourages these young people to stay and contribute in their new-found homes for the long-term. Over a nine-month period I was placed in six different organizations as a consultant, working for the federal and county governments, two small nonprofits, a private engineering firm, and on a successful mayoral campaign. I met over 200 leaders including CEOs of major companies, government officials, community members, and small business owners. The sixteen Coro Fellows began acting as a consulting firm, taking on clients and projects until our days stretched into sixteen-hour marathons without pause for months at a time. I personally interviewed the owner of the Pittsburgh Pirates and some of the highest ranking members of Congress—but also took a tour of an abandoned steel mill with a former blast furnace worker, waded through acid mine drainage during a flood crisis control effort, and packed medical supplies for impoverished nations in Africa. My experiences were diverse and intense. I have never been pushed as hard creatively, physically, and intellectually—but these experiences and leaders were not even my greatest sense of learning.

When surrounded for a year by fifteen other people with widely different perspectives and values than your own, who have worked as hard as you to participate in the program, and who become your colleagues, your business partners, and your friends—you have no choice but to learn. When people ask if Coro was fun, I often stumble for words remembering sleepless nights, deadlines galore, and frustrating meetings attempting to build consensus with fifteen amazing yet different people. But I smile knowing how much I learned in a short time. The ability to see the world from multiple perspectives is a valuable skill, developed most strongly through my time with other Coro fellows.

Studying full-time towards a master's in public policy while working for a small nonprofit seems easy in comparison to Coro. I will soon graduate from Carnegie Mellon University and consider the next steps in my life. Having directed the environmental initiatives at a community development organization in a low-income Pittsburgh neighborhood for over a year now, I am putting the skills I learned through Coro to use every day. I hope to contribute to Pittsburgh's Renaissance as I continue to learn and immerse myself in new experiences. Continuing to work with neighborhoods, pushing the boundaries of environmental innovation and education, and developing partnerships in new business ventures are all attainable goals because a supportive and creative advisor pushed me to try something "out of the box." From Villanova through Coro to now, there has always been one constant—the drive to learn.

Nate is a winner.

The value of the process. Yes, I have screamed at these words—but not for long. Actually, I have to smile when I think about the commitments our institutions have made to the nationally competitive scholarship process, and the benefits they have derived. Professionalizing scholarship advising, encouraging—and often funding—study abroad experiences for our students, supporting undergraduate research are investments that our schools have made. As a result of these initiatives, the growing culture of scholarship and leadership on our campuses has enhanced the reputations of each of our institutions within the academic community. For foundations, these commitments have resulted in increased numbers of highly qualified candidates in each of the competitions and, therefore, have elevated the level of expectations for scholar selection. More competition—more *genuine* competition—raises the bar. I smile when I think of how our students have matured from the opportunities that are now available to them—actually, *all* of our students, not just scholarship candidates. Participation in the scholarship application process is really the culminating event of a college experience in which the candidates come to know themselves as the caretakers and policy drivers of the next generation. These students are going out into a world that desperately needs them, and they are committed to improving the lives of others, particularly the most vulnerable. It is important for us to realize that regardless of whether or not they win a Marshall or a Rhodes, a Mitchell or a Gates Cambridge, they have achieved something far greater. And that, quite frankly, is winning of the highest order.

7

Helping Faculty Write Better Recommendation Letters

JOE SCHALL

Joe Schall is a writing tutor and the Giles Writer-in-Residence for Penn State's College of Earth and Mineral Sciences. His books include Writing Recommendation Letters: A Faculty Handbook *and* Writing Personal Statements and Scholarship Application Essays: A Student Handbook. *His articles have appeared in publications including* Writers' Forum (U.K.) *and* Academe. *He has won numerous awards for his fiction, including an Individual Creative Artists Fellowship in Literature from the Pennsylvania Council on the Arts and the Bobst Award for Emerging Writers from New York University. His short stories have appeared in journals including* The Baltimore Review *and* Indiana Review.

When the subject of writing recommendation letters is raised with faculty, an interesting thing often happens—they tell stories. These stories might be about a letter they wrote for a student, generously peppered with "creative exaggerations" to improve the student's credentials, or about a student who was too pushy about requesting a letter and refused to take "no" for an answer, or even about a letter they wrote to recommend *themselves* at the request of their department head. As such stories demonstrate, how we approach the process of writing letters of recommendation teaches us lessons about personal relationships, protocol, and our professional ethics as writers. Almost all faculty write recommendation letters on a regular basis, yet we rarely if ever receive formal training about the process, we worry about quality in letter writing and wonder about benchmarks for comparison, and we also rarely find opportunity to formally discuss the ethical concerns we wrestle with when writing letters.

In researching this topic, I have found that there is ample material in the literature—dating back about a century—to frame a discussion for the ethical, practical, and stylistic standards by which we write and judge quality in recommendation letters.[1] I explore these standards and offer examples of letters in the second edition of my book *Writing Recommendation Letters: A Faculty Handbook,* as well as discuss principles of writing letters for particular national scholarships, such as the Rhodes, Truman, and Jack Kent Cooke.[2] Further, in working with faculty in workshops on recommendation letter writing, I have found that they respond with vigor and express a desire for self-improvement, especially if the workshop gives them opportunity to air their concerns about letter writing and learn from the experiences of others.

Here, I discuss a three-part approach that can be taken when offering a workshop designed to help faculty improve their skills in writing recommendation letters for their students. In the first part, I recommend a brief historical and research-based snapshot of recommendation letter writing, with a focus on the common ethical and practical dilemmas for both writers and readers. Secondly, I recommend that faculty members are given the opportunity to discuss freely how they might respond to specific student cases, drawing on their own experiences as letter writers as they frame their responses. Finally, I suggest that faculty are given specific tips about improving their letter writing, so that they leave a workshop on the subject with a concrete sense of having learned something from their participation.

Recommendation Letters: A Brief Historical Perspective

Although most articles have emerged within the last forty years, over the past century about eighty articles on the subject of writing recommendation letters have appeared in journals ranging from *The Chronicle of Higher Education* to *Journal of Applied Psychology* to *Journal of Surgical Research.*[3] Articles in the *Chronicle* are often largely anecdotal, with writers discussing how letters can be used by foes to carry out vendettas, pointing out parallels between inflated grades and inflationary rhetoric in letters, and even sounding calls to abandon the system entirely and pay outside reviewers. Some article writers strongly defend the need that even average students have for letters of praise, acknowledge that inflationary rhetoric exists, but that letters are critical nonetheless, insisting that letters teach us more about candidates than any other part of their application.[4]

More empirically based studies on the subject tend to look at large samples of letters and identify trends, concerning themselves with both academic and social issues. Typical concerns are with sexism, gender, and cross-cultural differences in writers, legal issues, exaggeration in letters, and grade inflation.[5] One of the weightiest studies of recommendation letter writing came in 2002, when the American Academy of Arts and Sciences published *Evaluation and the Academy: Are We Doing the Right Thing?* This extensive paper argues that the fundamental means we use to evaluate rising students—by quantitative measures such as grades and qualitative measures such as recommendation letters—have substantially changed over time, and that we need to consider a dual ethical responsibility, to both student and evaluator, both when assigning grades and when writing letters.[6]

When discussing the topic of recommendation letter writing with faculty, citing material such as that just described validates both the academic and personal relevance of the subject, and such material also introduces the strong ethical component inherent in the process. These examples can be furthered through a simple poll of faculty workshop participants, with questions such as the following being considered:

1. How many have written at least twenty recommendation letters? Fifty? One Hundred? Hundreds?
2. How many have written an openly negative letter that could have harmed the candidate's chances?
3. How many fear making any negative comments in recommendation letters?
4. How many have turned down requests to write letters?

5. How many have seen any recommendation letters written on your behalf?
6. How many have been asked to write letters for yourself?

Such questions both set context for later discussion and signal to faculty that their experiences are relevant and useful to others. Even in a small group of faculty, inevitably there will be those who have written many letters and those who have written just a few. There may be faculty who have never turned down a request to write a letter or never written even a nuanced negative comment, and they welcome the chance to discuss with other faculty how they manage such tasks.

Finally, a humorous and interesting way to close the first part of a faculty workshop is to cite two studies on recommendation letter written about seventy years ago. In the 1930s, two theses were completed on the subject of recommendation letters as evaluative tools. The thesis *A Scale of Evaluation of School Administrators' Letters of Recommendation for Teachers* was written by Frank Evans Berkheimer in 1936.[7] Note the high level of candor in these excerpts from some of the letters cited in that study:

> "Some people in this section have questioned her deportment on certain occasions. . . . I feel that she might do better work in another community."
>
> "Miss N came to us a year ago. She has been in three different systems in the four years of her experience. . . . We don't feel that we should prevent Miss N from continuing her annual change."
>
> "His pupils are fairly well interested in their work, but never excel. I believe you could procure his services at his present salary."
>
> "She is married but her husband is not with her. . . . If she were not my sister, I would like to speak of her in detail."
>
> "Please destroy this letter when you have read it."

Obvious humor and irony aside, these comments are interesting because they show just how much things have changed in our evaluative practices over time. Today, one would rarely find such comments in letters, partly because the letter writers would fear legal action or other repercussions for their honesty. Certainly, evaluators would be shocked to receive some of these comments by today's standards.

In contrast, when we consider the problems we have in relation to recommendation letters today, we find that these problems are not at all new.

A 1935 thesis by Lloyd Morrisett,[8] entitled *Letters of Recommendation: A Study of Letters of Recommendation as an Instrument in the Selection of Secondary School Teachers,* summed up the problems of both writing and evaluating quality in recommendation letters as follows:

1. The writer of testimonials and letters of recommendation is likely to view his task lightly.
2. The writer for mere accommodation will often exceed his knowledge or falsify it.
3. There is no way of checking against errors.
4. Bias or carelessness of the writer is a factor.
5. The writer may overstate or underestimate the case of the candidate.
6. The writer may simply make inadequate statements perfunctory in character.

This brief historical look, then, gives faculty the opportunity to put their problems relevant to letter writing in context and in perspective. Workshop participants begin to realize the universality of such issues as concerns over quality in letters, the nature of praise and criticism, fear of repercussions when we make negative comments, and the need for specifics over superficiality. These issues can be amplified for faculty through the consideration of specific student cases.

Using Student Cases to Frame Discussions on Recommendation Letter Writing

In giving workshops or leading discussions on recommendation letter writing, I have used three approaches: 1) several hours of lecture and discussion with faculty who are open to a "training session" on letter writing, complete with focused writing exercises; 2) an informal luncheon in which small groups discuss the issues at different tables with group facilitators; 3) a short lecture and discussion with both students and faculty, emphasizing how the two can partner on the writing process.

Unifying these three approaches is the use of cases. Student cases— detailed written scenarios involving a student requesting a letter of recommendation with some surmountable complication built into the scenario—work well with faculty for many reasons. They can be openly discussed within a small group without a strong sense of risk for the (hypothetical) student or evaluator, and thus they remind us of the ethical dilemmas we face as writers and encourage us to meet them head-on. By definition, student cases invite us to share "war stories" about our own students and circumstances, promoting spirited debate and a reinvigorated approach among faculty. When we participate in student case discussions, especially with seasoned faculty writers, we find that we generate ideas about content through discussion and share such information as time-saving strategies used by authors when writing letters. Ultimately, if student cases are presented well and taken seriously by workshop participants, they help faculty feel good about students and more empowered about letter writing.[9]

Built into the use of student cases should be the assumption that the faculty member genuinely does wish to help the student, but will have a particular challenge in doing so, else the faculty member might meet the challenge simply by opting out. Also, there should be an actual assignment for those considering the student case to complete, either individually or as a group. This way, faculty are urged toward pointed discussion with some end goal in mind. For instance, when I have presented cases in short workshops, I typically charge the faculty with the following two tasks:

1. Write at least one sentence that legitimately points out a limitation about the student (or the circumstances) but that would still be useful in a letter of recommendation.
2. Write at least one sentence of unqualified praise specific to the student and suitable for inclusion in a recommendation letter. Enhance credibility and utility of the praise through concrete detail that would be valued in the student's field.

What follows are three examples of cases that I have used in faculty workshops, often accompanied by pictures of the hypothetical students (downloaded from a website such as fotostock.com) to help humanize them.

CASE: Rafael

Rafael was enrolled in your Introduction to Bioinformatics class two years ago. In the course of just a few hours—ironically, while you are attending a faculty development luncheon on writing recommendation letters—Rafael sends you four e-mails asking you for a letter of recommendation. Two of the e-mails issue corrections to mistakes made in previous e-mails, and the final e-mail includes an attachment—allegedly Rafael's resume—which your computer cannot open. One of his e-mails poses four questions, including "What is a personal statement, and how do I write one?" Rafael gives you a deadline of one week in which to write the letter and asks you to e-mail it back to him when you're finished with it. He does not specify what the letter is for—just that he would like you to write one. While you read his e-mails, he sends you a fifth e-mail warning you that one of his previous e-mails may have contained a virus.

You at first recall Rafael by name only, then retreat to your records to find that he received a C+ in your class (and the + was a gift), and suddenly you recall him very well, in that he was highly popular amongst his classmates and known for playing in a bluegrass band popular at the local bars. In fact, you recall that he persuaded you to donate fifty dollars to a "Battle of the Bands" benefit concert and sent you a handwritten thank you card and chocolate bar afterward. You remember that he has a jovial, winning, self-effacing manner despite his obvious limitations at both cyberspace etiquette and academics.

CASE: Tasha

You are the advisor for the Advertising Club on campus, and in that context you have come to know Tasha, who breezily refers to herself as a "clubber" because she is involved in over a dozen campus clubs. You think well of Tasha because of her obvious devotion and energy, but you know that she is an average student whose academic life seems to take second place to her other activities. In fact, Tasha once said to you, with half-seriousness, that the school should have a major in extracurricular activities. Tasha is also involved in the campus animal rights group, which staged a successful protest against serving *foie gras* at a local restaurant, and you recall that at a recent Christmas party the club's advisor—one of your best friends—referred to Tasha as a "gadfly" who "stirs things up." You were just a tad tipsy at the party, and you're fuzzy about whether there are any positive connotations to the word "gadfly."

After first setting up an appointment, Tasha has respectfully approached you in your office to ask you for what she loosely calls a "character reference." She is only a sophomore, but has broad plans to work for some sort of activist organization after graduation, and she asks you to write her an all-purpose letter that she can carry with her to potential employers in the future. She likes to "plan ahead." She tells you that the advisor for the campus animal rights group is also a potential reference, but that you know her much better than that advisor does.

CASE: Jonathan

You are an assistant professor in your second year, and you have written just four recommendation letters in your life. Despite your limited experience, it's obvious that Jonathan is one of the best undergrads you will ever know. He is clearly headed for graduate school and has excelled in the honors program. His accomplishments in college are stunning, and have included his production of a twenty-minute documentary film on a local spring, an award of a Udall Scholarship his sophomore year, and a special citation from the local Red Cross for volunteer work in a blood drive. Jonathan shows you his resume, which is six pages long, and asks you to write a letter of recommendation for a graduate NSF grant. He chooses you as a recommender simply because he adores your class, which he is taking in his senior year "just for fun."

Jonathan's major is chemistry, and his twin passions are toxicology and genetic engineering. His graduate plans are highly focused, and he has even corresponded with a faculty member at his target school. He excitedly tells you he wants to study reproduction in the Japanese Medaka fish, which are "way cool 'cause they ovulate daily." He whimsically dreams of someday genetically engineering a transgenic fish that fluoresces when it ovulates, and sees it as a potentially big money maker. You teach a general education course in Greco-Roman religions.

FACULTY RESPONSES TO STUDENT CASES

Of course, how well faculty "play the assigned role" in a student case matters little—the point is to engage them in a debate and discussion of how best to respond to the case before them, and to help them begin to compose a letter specific to the student.

In workshops that I have witnessed where the previous student cases were used, faculty have often strongly defended the student (while some have even attacked the student) or their own position, and they have delighted in coming up with creative wording for criticisms in particular.[10]

Under the assumption that they do indeed wish to help the student, they will generally agree that Rafael is a likeable enough figure but that his average performance should be reflected in his letter, that Tasha's unrealized potential and boundless energy may just need to be nurtured a bit to come to fruition, and that neither Jonathan's whimsical dreams nor his stellar accomplishments should be evaluated in a way that the faculty member is either too skeptical or too gushy.

Finally, group discussion of these student cases helps faculty realize that they can and should sometimes massage the circumstances of the student request—that is, advise the student about the very nature of recommendation letters, develop more of a relationship with the student in order to write a letter of maximum efficacy, or find out more about such issues as who the student's other recommenders are, so that the faculty member's recommendation letter can be positive but appropriately limited in scope. As noted earlier, the goal is to help faculty feel more empowered and informed about letter writing, and to embrace a re-invigorated approach to the task.

Giving Faculty Materials to Help Them Improve Their Letter Writing

The final suggested part of a faculty workshop on recommendation letter writing is some sort of resource—a set of tips or an article or handbook that will encourage further study of the subject and promote positive change. What follows are five of the tips that I have shared with faculty as part of a handout to end the workshop.

1. In the right circumstances, consider saying "no" to the request to write a letter and devote your energy to other letters you should be writing.

   Good reasons to say "no":
   - Your support of or knowledge about the student doesn't match the weight of the opportunity.
   - For reasons of time, temperament, or because you have a performance-specific reason not to support the student, you're not inclined to write a letter.

- The student approaches you in such an unprofessional manner that you cannot in good conscience endorse the student.

2. When writing letters, avoid the most common and most harmful mistakes.

Common mistakes writers make in recommendation letters:
- Poorly presented material, even to the point of irrelevancy, or seeming incompetence because of poor grammar or multiple spelling errors.
- A visible lack of necessary information about the scholarship or opportunity for which the student is applying.
- A generic "boilerplate" letter with no specifics about the student.
- A letter praising the student beyond credibility, or praising in a way that is not backed up with parallel qualitative or quantitative examples.
- Potentially discriminatory comments, especially those directly related to race, gender, sexual orientation, appearance, or any handicapping condition.
- Seemingly "coded" language or seeming criticism through obvious omission of expected information.

3. To enhance your credibility and aid the evaluator in making assessments, use both praise and criticism effectively.

Effective praise:
- Avoids hyperbole and cliché.
- Is tied to specifics about the student, perhaps citing a student's paper or exam performance.
- Is linked directly to appropriate evaluative criteria.
- Doesn't reach beyond the scope of the writer's experience.

Effective criticism:
- Can be tied directly to the express desire of selectors for honest criticism.
- Is often limited to one sentence or paragraph.
- May have already been shared with the student—a fact perhaps noted in the letter.
- May cite the writer's ethic of being a holistic evaluator.

4. Partner with the student on the process and establish an appropriate, instructive protocol for your interactions.

   Positive ways to partner with students on letter writing:
   - Review the student's resume and personal statement, mining these documents for material to include in your letter.

   - Interview the student for ten to fifteen minutes about future plans and take notes for your letter.

   - Have students "teach you" about the scholarship or program to which they're applying.

   - Ask who the other evaluators are and what the substance of their commentary is likely to be.

   - Decide if and how you want to use e-mail contact with the student, and stick to the rules you establish.

   - Invite students to do a self-evaluation of their strengths and weaknesses, perhaps even in writing.

5. Study models, read and write articles on the subject of letter writing, educate yourself on national scholarships, and re-evaluate your own practices.

   A few ideas for studying the art of recommendation letter writing:
   - *The Chronicle of Higher Education* includes numerous articles on the subject of recommendation letter writing, in particular in the "First Person" section.[11]

   - Articles about letter writing may already exist within your discipline—even psychology journals and medical journals have included such articles.[12]

   - Any faculty member might undertake a small study on the subject, perhaps internally within one's department, or write an article about recommendation letters to even a small but widely distributed publication such as *The Teaching Professor.*[13]

   - The 2002 publication *Evaluation and the Academy: Are We Doing the Right Thing?* (the American Academy of Arts and Sciences) is worth reading and sharing with colleagues.[14]

- The second edition of Joe Schall's *Writing Recommendation Letters: A Faculty Handbook,* includes discussion of ethical, practical, and stylistic issues, information on national scholarships, and models for study.[15]

The approach described in this essay has served me well in conducting faculty workshops on recommendation letter writing because it taps into the desire of participants to share war stories, respond to practical and humanizing student cases, and come away armed with ideas and resources. The schools where I have conducted these workshops have ranged from Roanoke to Holy Cross to Marist, and at every school participants have responded with enthusiasm and optimism. I think faculty members genuinely welcome the opportunity to reflect on this critical task that they perform on a regular basis but for which they receive no formal training. Giving them opportunities to talk about writing recommendation letters allows them to consider the issues from a fresh perspective, and ultimately helps them help the population we all serve—our students.

8

International Students
A Case for More Advisor Support

CAMILLE STILLWELL

Camille Stillwell coordinates the National Scholarships Office at the University of Maryland, College Park, which she established in 1999. She is a founding member of the National Association of Fellowships Advisors and was a co-presenter on the topic of International Students and National Scholarships at the 2005 NAFA Conference in Louisville, Kentucky. Ms. Stillwell has served on national selection committees for the James Madison Fellowship, the Jacob Javits Fellowship, and the Orphan Foundation.

It's that awful moment—perhaps during office hours, perhaps at a scholarship workshop. A student asks, "I am from [FILL IN COUNTRY], and not a U.S. citizen. Can I apply for this scholarship? If not, are there any scholarships that you are aware of that I can apply for?" The problem is that many advisors rarely think about scholarships for international students and are not prepared to respond to this inquiry. The response to such a question is all too often the usual psychosomatic reactions to stress—tight throat, dry mouth, sweaty palms, the overwhelming desire to flee. . . .

At the 2005 National Association of Fellowship Advisors Conference on *National Scholarships and International Students*, Sharon Chambers-Gordon and I presented a workshop on advising international students. Afterward, several advisors shared with me that they are at a loss on advising international students. Some admit that they try to avoid these students as best they can. A typical advising method is to refer them to a few online search engines with the hope that they do not return for more information. This is, unfortunately, a very limited view of what I see as a relatively untapped scholarship group. Scholarship advisors need to take a more positive, proactive look at encouraging international students to become more actively involved in national scholarship competitions.

International students with scholarship potential have the same basic attributes as aspiring American students with scholarship promise. A few adjectives describe these students collectively—they are intelligent, ambitious, focused, and determined to succeed. Many within this group have interesting stories to tell and/or have overcome obstacles in order to excel in higher education. Beyond these basic attributes, however, the path to identifying and properly preparing international students for national scholarship competitions may be fraught with obstacles—language and cultural barriers and educational differences that can result in a reluctance among international students to pursue competitive opportunities.

Here are the facts. Recent data from *Open Doors 2006: International Students in the United States* indicate that enrollment of foreign students are on the rise.[1] There are over half a million foreign students in the United States, the largest group of students (over fifty-eight percent) coming from Asian countries, primarily India, Mainland China, Korea, and Japan. Students from these traditional cultures tend to feel "distant to the American culture," making it difficult for them to approach faculty or staff for scholarship advising because they feel intimidated by the process.

Go Tell It to the Mountain

At the University of Maryland, I try to bridge international students' sense of distance by attending events that are hosted by our office of International Education Services (IES). Every semester, I sponsor an International Coffee Hour event where I provide scholarship information to international students. Not only do they come for food and fellowship, they get an opportunity to hear critical information about scholarship opportunities, the value of the process, and strategies for being competitive. I often start my presentation by acknowledging that I am an older "new American" (I hail from a small country in the Caribbean), and I do in some part understand some of the challenges that they may be experiencing. Their ability to meet me in their comfort zone has encouraged many future one-on-one visits to my office. There, I can address their individual concerns with aspects of the scholarship process such as approaching faculty for reference letters and utilizing resources on campus such as the Writing Center if language is an issue.

Show Me the Money

To demystify the search process, I have made it a policy with all scholarship marketing materials that I produce and at every scholarship workshop that I conduct, by including the phrase "Open to International Students" where applicable. In this way, students know upfront whether or not it is a scholarship opportunity that they can fully explore. Nothing is as frustrating for international students than to receive information that they cannot pursue. In addition, over the past few years, I have dedicated a scholarship web page for international students (*http://www.scholarships.umd.edu/internationalstudent. html*) with data gathered from embassies as well as an alphabetized list of funding opportunities. And, for those who want to search further, there is another web page with search engines that provide scholarship information for non-U.S. students. Databases such as Community of Science (*http:// fundingopps.cos.com/*) are excellent tools that allow searches based on nationality and/or residency.

Can These Students Win National Scholarships?

Nothing inspires students more than knowing about their peers who have been successful in national scholarship competitions. This is certainly the case with international students. It adds the one dimension that we tend to overlook with this group—it is that they are just as *deserving* of a national scholarship as any other high achieving student. Pictures and information of our international students who are Jack Kent Cooke

Scholarship recipients have been an inspiration for our current international scholarship hopefuls. Our Jack Kent Cooke scholars represent every corner of the globe, hailing from Australia, Bolivia, India, Ethiopia, and more.

I urge advisors to take on a new perspective when you are advising an international student about national scholarship opportunities. Make that first step. Go beyond cultural and language differences to see their scholarship potential. Provide these students with scholarship information from the moment they arrive on your campuses with orientation scholarship brochures or flyers. Collaborate with international groups on scholarship presentations. Encourage these students to develop strong relationships with faculty. Start early by encouraging international students to create and build on their curriculum vitae, discover their passions beyond the classroom, and explore research options. In essence, take away the word "international," and what remains are stellar, deserving students with scholarship potential, worthy of our time, commitment, and scholarship expertise.

Selected Funding Opportunities Open to Non-U.S. Citizens

A. Patrick Charnon Memorial Scholarship
http://www.cesresources.org/charnon.html
Full-time undergraduate students enrolled in a four-year college in the United States. Each scholarship carries a stipend of $1,500 per academic year. Recipients may re-apply each year for up to four years, provided they continue to meet the requirements of the award. Applications accepted January 15–August 1.

All-U.S.A. College Academic Team
http://www.usatoday.com/news/education/default.htm
Recognition program for exceptional full-time undergraduates at four-year institutions in the U.S.A. and its territories. Deadline: Late November.

Allen Lee Hughes Fellowship
http://www.arena-stage.org/about/employment/fellows
Individuals interested in artistic and technical production, arts administration, and community engagement. Fellowship provides a modest stipend. Deadline: April 1.

Amelia Earhart Fellowships (Zonta International Foundation)
http://www.zonta.org/site/PageServer?pagename=zi_issues_programs_amelia_earhart
Women of any nationality with a superior academic record and a bachelor's degree in science or engineering. Fellowships carry a stipend of $6,000; approximately thirty-five are awarded annually. Deadline: mid-November.

American Association for University Women–International Fellowships
http://www.aauw.org/fga/fellowships_grants/international.cfm
Full-time study or research to women who are not U.S. citizens or permanent residents. Both graduate and postgraduate study at accredited institutions are supported. Deadline: December 1.

American Scandinavian Foundation
http://www.amscan.org/fellowship.html
Denmark, Finland, Iceland, Norway, or Sweden citizens for study or research programs (usually at the graduate level) in the United States for up to one year. Awards are made in all fields.

Asian Cultural Council
http://www.asianculturalcouncil.org/programs.html#acc
Individual fellowship grants to artists, scholars, students, and specialists from Asia for study, research, travel, and creative work in the United States. Deadlines vary.

Asian Development Bank (ADB)—Japan Scholarship Program
http://www.adb.org/JSP/default.asp
Citizens of ADB's developing member countries to pursue postgraduate studies in economics, management, science and technology, and other development-related fields at participating academic institutions in the Asian and Pacific Region. The ADB-JSP provides full scholarships for one to two years.

Association for Women in Science Educational Foundation
http://www.awis.org/about/fellows.html
Female students enrolled in a behavioral, life, physical, or social science, or engineering program leading to a Ph.D. degree. Graduate fellowships in the amount of $1,000 are awarded each year. Deadline: January.

Bibliographical Society of America Fellowship Program
http://www.bibsocamer.org/fellows.htm
Short-term fellowship program supporting bibliographical inquiry as well as research in the history of the book trades and in publishing history. Deadline: December.

Canon Collins Educational Trust
http://www.canoncollins.org.uk/
Full scholarship for nationals from southern African countries (South Africa, Namibia, Botswana, Swaziland, Lesotho, Zimbabwe, Zambia, Malawi, Angola, and Mozambique) who wish to pursue a postgraduate degree (normally a one year master's degree) in either the United Kingdom or southern Africa. Application deadlines: for the United Kingdom: Sept.–Dec., for southern Africa, August each year.

Carnegie Endowment for International Peace Junior Fellow Program
http://www.carnegieendowment.org/about/index.cfm?fa=jrFellows
Year-long paid internship for graduating seniors interested in careers in international affairs. Internship is at the Carnegie Endowment for World Peace in Washington, DC. Deadline: January 15.

Chevening Scholarship Program
http://www.chevening.com
Three different scholarship schemes for postgraduate study in the United Kingdom. For students from selected countries. Eligible for all fields of study. Deadlines vary depending on country.

Christine Mirzayan Science & Technology Policy Graduate Fellowship Program
http://www.nationalacademies.org/policyfellows/
Designed to engage graduate science, engineering, medical, veterinary, business, and law students in the analysis that informs the creation of science and technology policy and to familiarize them with the interactions of science, technology, and government.

Commonwealth Scholarship
http://www.acu.ac.uk/cusac/
Commonwealth citizens to pursue postgraduate study or doctoral study at Commonwealth universities. Deadlines vary by country.

Cosmos Club Foundation Grants in Aid to Young Scholars
http://www.consortium.org/cosmos_club_grants.asp
$1,500–$3,000 grants to meet specific research needs not covered by other supporting funds (e.g., small items of equipment [ordinarily expendable], special supplies, travel to research facilities, or to attend relevant meetings). Applicants must be enrolled in a program leading to a graduate degree (masters or doctoral) in a member institution of the Consortium of Universities of the Washington Metropolitan Area. Deadline: November.

DAAD Annual Grants
http://www.daad.org/?p=50407
Undergraduate scholarships to study in the Federal Republic of Germany. Foreign nationals are eligible if they are attending a U.S. institution for their undergraduate degree. Applications in all fields are accepted, with the exception of dentistry, medicine, pharmacy, and veterinary medicine. Deadlines vary.

Davis-Putter Scholarships
http://www.davisputter.org/
Need-based grants (up to $6,000) to undergraduate or graduate students actively working for peace and justice on campus and/or in the community. Deadline: April 1.

Echoing Green Public Service Fellowships
http://www.echoinggreen.org
Funding to conduct public service projects anywhere in the world. For up to two years of support.

Edmund S. Muskie Ph.D. Fellowship
http://www.muskiefoundation.org/fellowships.html
Twenty-two fellowships for doctoral-level programs in business administration, economics, public administration, and public policy. For citizens of Georgia, Russia, or Ukraine.

Elie Wiesel Prize in Ethics
http://www.eliewieselfoundation.org/EthicsPrize/information.html
Essay contest for full-time juniors or seniors. Prizes range from $500–$5,000. Deadline: December.

Elizabeth Greenshields Foundation Grant for Artists
http://www.calarts.edu/~stdafrs/web/greenshields.html
$10,000 (Canadian) award for talented artists. No age limit. Not for those pursuing abstract or nonrepresentational art.

Environmental Research and Education Foundation
http://www.erefdn.org/scholar.html
This scholarship recognizes excellence in Ph.D. or post-doctoral environmental research and education. Deadline: May 1.

Eurasian Undergraduate Exchange Program (UGRAD)
http://www.irex.org/programs/ugrad/index.asp
Fellowships to first-, second-, and third-year undergraduate students from Armenia, Azerbaijan, Belarus, Georgia, Kazakhstan, Kyrgyzstan, Moldova, Russian Federation, Tajikistan, Turkmenistan, Ukraine, and Uzbekistan. This program supports one year of non-degree undergraduate study in the United States in the fields of accounting, agriculture, American studies, business, computer science, criminal justice, economics, education, environmental management, hospitality management, international relations, journalism and mass communication, law, political science, psychology, and sociology. Deadline: November.

Exploration Fund of the Explorers Club
http://explorers.org/resources/funding/funding.php
$1,200 grants in support of exploration and field research. Funds given primarily to graduate students.

Fulbright
http://www.iie.org/FulbrightTemplate.cfm?Section=Foreign_Student_Program
Educational exchanges that strengthen understanding and communication between the United States and over students from 140 countries. Students interested in applying for the Fulbright Student Program must apply through the Fulbright Program Office in their home country.

Gates Cambridge Scholarships
http://www.gates.scholarships.cam.ac.uk/
One to three years of study in any discipline at Cambridge University. Candidates apply directly through Cambridge. Deadline: mid to late October.

Glamour Magazine's Top Ten College Women Competition
$1,500 cash award to outstanding juniors. Contact: ttcw@glamour.com
for more information.

Goldman Sachs Global Leaders Program
*http://www.gs.com/our_firm/our_culture/social_responsibility/gs_foundation/
index.html*
$3,000 award for 100 outstanding second year college students in any field
of study.

Hellenic Times Scholarship Fund
http://www.htsfund.org/guidelines.html
For undergraduate and graduate students of Greek descent, between the
ages of seventeen and twenty-five. Deadline: January.

Herbert Scoville Jr. Peace Fellowships
http://www.scoville.org/apply.html
Internship opportunity for college graduates to serve six to nine months
with a participating organization of their choice in Washington DC.
Deadlines vary.

Humane Studies Fellowships
http://www.theihs.org/scholarships
For undergraduate and graduate students interested in the classical liberal/
libertarian tradition of individual rights and market economies. More than
100 fellowships up to $12,000 are awarded annually. Deadline: late
December.

Inter American Press Association (IAPA) Scholarship
http://www.sipiapa.org/otheractivities/scholarships.cfm
For young journalists and journalism school graduates from Canada,
Latin America, the Caribbean, and the United States. Deadline:
December 31.

International Dissertation Field Research Fellowships
http://www.ssrc.org/programs/idrf/
Up to fifty fellowships to support social scientists and humanists
conducting dissertation field research in all areas and regions of the
world.

Irex Small Grants Fund for the Middle East and North Africa
http://www.irex.org/programs/MENA_grants.asp
Grants between $2,500 and $10,000 for projects to support civil society organizations, education professionals, media, and journalists in the Middle East and North Africa. Deadline: June.

ISA Educational Foundation Scholarships
http://www.isa.org/Content/NavigationMenu/General_Information/careers/Scholarships/Scholarships.htm
Various scholarships for students in the fields of automation and control. Deadline: February.

J. W. Saxe Memorial Fund
http://www.jwsaxefund.org/memorialfund.html
Annual $1,000 scholarship to one or more undergraduate or graduate students working in public service. Deadline: March.

Jack Kent Cooke Graduate Scholarships
http://www.jackkentcookefoundation.org/
Graduating seniors or recent alumni. Open to all fields of study at any accredited university in the US or abroad. Award is up to $50,000 per year for up to six years. Deadline: late April.

Japan-IMF Scholarship Program for Advanced Studies
http://www.imf.org/external/np/ins/english/scholar.htm
Nationals of IMF Asian member countries interested in studying for their doctorates in economics in order to work in an international financial institution (such as the IMF or the World Bank) or in their home administrations. Deadline: December 31.

John Bayliss Radio Scholarship
http://www.baylissfoundation.org/radio.html
15 Scholarships for juniors, seniors, and graduate level students majoring in Broadcast Communications. Deadline: March.

Joint Japan/World Bank Graduate Scholarship Regular Program
http://worldbank.org/
Click on Learning, then on Scholarships. For individuals from World Bank member countries to undertake graduate studies at any university located in a World Bank member country except their own. Suggested

fields of study: economics, public administration, finance, planning, health, population, agriculture, infrastructure, information systems and aquatic resources (provided that the focus of study is on public policy aspects of these fields), environment and natural resource management, education, and other development-related subjects. Deadline: March 31.

Josephine de Karman Scholarships
http://www.dekarman.org
$16,000 scholarship to support either the final year of study for juniors or for PhD candidates with ABD status. Deadline: late January.

Kate Neal Kinley Memorial Fellowship
http://www.faa.uiuc.edu/about_faa/funding_opportunities.html
Annual fellowship for advanced study of Fine Arts in the United States or abroad, to enhance professional standing or to finance a special project. Preference for candidates under twenty-five years. There are three fellowships of $7,500 each in art, architecture or music; an additional music fellowship for $15,000; and up to three alternate awards of up to $1,000 each. Deadline: mid-January.

King Faisal Foundation Scholarship
http://www.kff.com/english/Scholarships/ScholarshipsIndex.html
Funding opportunity for Muslim students in medicine, engineering, and sciences (physics, chemistry, and geology) to study at an accredited European or North American university.

Microsoft Scholarships
http://www.microsoft.com/college/ss_overview.mspx
Four types of scholarships for undergraduate students interested in computer science and related technical disciplines. One-year award for students attending institutions in the United States, Canada, and Mexico. All recipients of a scholarship will be required to complete a salaried summer internship of 12 weeks or more at Microsoft Corporation in Redmond, Washington. Deadline: mid-January.

Nelson Mandela Scholarships
http://www.nelsonmandelascholarship.co.za
Up to fourteen scholarships offered for disadvantaged South African students to pursue postgraduate study in the United Kingdom. Deadline: mid-November.

Olive W. Garvey Fellowships
http://www.independent.org/students/garvey
Biennial award to outstanding college students around the world through a competitive essay contest on the meaning and significance of economic and personal liberty. Awards range from $1,000 to $2,500. Deadline: May.

Organization of American States (OAS) Fellowships
http://www.educoas.org/portal/en/becas/acerca.aspx?culture= en&tabindex= 44&childindex= 45
For graduate study or research in any field except medical sciences or introductory language study. Deadlines vary.

Overseas Research Students Award Scheme
http://www.universitiesuk.ac.uk/ors
Funding to pay the difference between international student fees and home EU fees for international students at U.K. institutions.

Peace Scholar Dissertation Fellowship
http://www.usip.org/fellows/scholars.html
Supports doctoral dissertations that explore the sources and nature of international conflict, and strategies to prevent or end conflict and to sustain peace. Citizens of all countries are eligible, but must be enrolled in an accredited college or university in the United States. Deadline: January.

Rhodes Scholarships for Non-U.S. Citizens
http://www.rhodesscholar.org
One to three years of study at Oxford University for citizens of Australia, Bangladesh, Bermuda, Canada, Commonwealth Caribbean and Jamaica, Germany, Hong Kong, India, Kenya, Malaysia, New Zealand, Pakistan, Singapore, South Africa, Uganda, Zambia, and Zimbabwe. Open to all fields. Deadlines vary.

The Roothbert Fund Scholarship Program
http://www.roothbertfund.org/scholarships.php
Approximately twenty ($2,000–$3,000) awards are offered to students in the United States in need of financial aid to further their education at the undergraduate or graduate level. Deadline: early February.

Rotary International Ambassadorial Scholarships
http://www.rotary.org/foundation/educational/amb_schol/prospect/index.html

One-year study abroad opportunity in any discipline in over 160 countries worldwide. Deadlines vary by district.

Rotary Peace Scholarships
http://www.rotary.org/foundation/educational/amb_scho/centers/application/index.html
Funding to support two-year master's-level degree program at one of the Rotary Centers for International Studies. Seventy scholarships are offered worldwide. Deadlines vary by Rotary district.

Russian Young Leadership Fellows for Public Service Program
http://www.irex.org/
One year of non-degree academic study at leading universities and colleges throughout the United States. Fellows concentrate on community, governmental, or corporate affairs.

Samuel Huntington Public Service Fellowship Award
http://www.nationalgridus.com/masselectric/about_us/award.asp
Annual stipend of $10,000 for a graduating college senior to pursue public service anywhere in the world. Deadline: mid February.

Seaspace Scholarships
http://www.seaspace.org
Supports marine-related courses of study for undergraduate students entering their junior or senior years and graduate students with an overall GPA of at least 3.3/4.0 and demonstrating financial need. Deadline: February.

Society of Women Engineers
http://www.societyofwomenengineers.org/scholarships/brochure.aspx
Various awards for women pursuing baccalaureate or graduate degrees in engineering or computer science, as well as engineering and computer science students enrolled in ABET-accredited engineering programs. Deadlines vary.

South Pacific and East Timor Scholarship Programs
http://pidp.eastwestcenter.org/pidp/
Two special degree study programs for citizens of South Pacific nations and East Timor. Scholarships are awarded for undergraduate degree study. Priority is given to applicants seeking degrees that address national development needs.

9

A Path Revealed
Reflections of a Former Scholarship Advisor

MARY HALE TOLAR

*Mary Hale Tolar, a Truman Scholar (1988) and a Rhodes Scholar (1990),
has established and directed postgraduate scholarship programs at the
University of Tulsa and Willamette University, and worked closely with the
scholarship programs at George Washington and Kansas State Universities.
In early 1999, she began serving as the deputy executive secretary of the
Truman Scholarship Foundation and was the first to suggest the possibility of
an organization that would have as its membership postgraduate scholarship
advisors. She is a founding member of NAFA and was its inaugural
Foundation Liaison. She now serves as the associate director for Civic
Leadership at Kansas State University.*

The story in my family goes . . . when I was five years old, I asked my
dad (then a forty-year-old minister) what he wanted to be when he
grew up. He smiled, thought about it, and said, "I don't know. But I like
figuring it out." What a gift he gave me. Early on, I learned it was about
the journey. (This story also shows that I was in training to be a scholarship

advisor before I had fully entered grade school—asking people to think about what they wanted to do . . . to find their path . . . who knew?)

I was drawn professionally to scholarship advising because of personal experience. As an undergraduate, I applied for several national scholarships and had the great fortune of working with Nancy Twiss. I had a great education at K-State. I learned from knowledgeable faculty who were invested in my academic growth. Caring administrators and staff provided students opportunities to cultivate and demonstrate leadership. But it was the scholarship process that shaped my college experience. Nancy Twiss steadily, earnestly, and with great grace guided me through a process, grounded in a series of questions that helped me determine both my "grand plan," and my next steps. The questions, simply put, are: Who am I? What do I care about? What kind of contribution do I want to make in this world? How am I going to get there?

These four questions, which I've asked students throughout my career, were recently asked of me. More accurately, I challenged myself to review all four as I considered a career change. The path I've taken, unintentional as I thought it was, has led me to a most logical, rational place. More importantly, it is the RIGHT place.

What attracted me to scholarship advising—assisting a student with the process of charting a course at a critical time—remains a strong pull. But it had always niggled at me because the process though so valuable is really open to a select few given the nature of the competitions. It never seemed . . . right? Fair? No, not that. It never seemed *enough*. I do not propose that the scholarship process change, or that all scholarship advisors should now advise all students regardless of fit to the competitions. This is not a critique on what is an unapologetically elite enterprise. There is value and purpose in the composition and execution of nationally competitive scholarships. I fully recognize and appreciate that. And yet . . .

We know that the "worthy many" of qualified, competitive scholarship candidates who are not selected as the "lucky few" doesn't even scratch the surface. The process benefited these students, certainly; but it did not reward them. What then about all the other engaged students on our campuses that, for any number of reasons, would never enter the office of a scholarship advisor? These are students who would also clearly benefit from the structured advising process founded on reflective, focused responses to critical questions.

So after many moves and many jobs, I moved home. I am back to where my understanding of higher education took shape. I care deeply about my *alma mater,* Kansas State University. It is a special place. I know others feel much the same about their alma maters, so every graduate will understand that when I say K-State is the best university *ever,* that I speak the truth, as I know it. Of course, I'd like to think that I have some perspective; I have worked at four other institutions, and visited numerous campuses across the country in my days with the Truman Foundation and as a consultant. K-State is a warm and welcoming place where excellence is fostered, cultivated, and rewarded—as is service, civility, collaboration, and compassion. And a remarkable thing has been happening here.

Ten years ago, with the vision of: a dean of students who believed leadership could be learned; the entrepreneurial spirit of Dr. Susan Scott, then associate dean of students, and Dr. Robert Shoop, a member of the faculty in Educational Leadership; the support of senior administrators and the wider campus community developed during a year-long task force; and, of course, approval of the Kansas Board of Regents, an academic minor in leadership was established. Leadership Studies and Programs Director Dr. Susan M. Scott and Professor and Senior Scholar Dr. Robert Shoop created a program focused on twin goals of personal development and the academic, interdisciplinary study of leadership. The program provides access to significant leadership development opportunities. The opportunities had been present when I was a student; student leadership is a hallmark of K-State culture. But what the program provided was *access.* Through the eighteen-credit hour academic minor, available to all K-State undergraduates, students in Leadership Studies and Programs tap into a process of both academic study and self-discovery, and step also into the practice of leadership. In ten years, the minor in leadership studies is the largest academic program at K-State, with over 1,500 students.

Now, I am a person who is comfortable with and has been rewarded for traditional academic study. I have been trained to view "leadership" skeptically—particularly as a discipline within the academy—and frankly, encouraged to view "all-things-student-affairs" warily as well. We all know there is rigor, and there is fluff, right? What I discovered at K-State was clearly a program of substance and worth, a program that had operationalized for the broader student body the principles of the scholarship process. Oh yes. I was home.

As associate director for Civic Leadership within Leadership Studies and Programs, I focus on service learning, community service, and civic engagement opportunities for students. I also teach the capstone course in the minor, the Senior Seminar. The final for this course is a personal statement— of no more than a thousand words, where students must address the following core questions: Who am I? Who do I want to be? What kind of contribution do I want to make, and how? Why am I ready to lead?

My path brought me home to K-State and to Leadership Studies and Programs, where I am able to contribute pieces of the scholarship process, a process I have valued so highly for so long, to students from all academic disciplines, regardless of academic rank. I contribute to preparing leaders at all levels and in all sectors of society—active, informed, citizens. Could it get any better? To quote my father, now a seventy-five-year-old retired pastor and active storyteller, "I don't know. But I like figuring it out."

10

The Truman Scholar Community
Unconventional Students Serving the Public Good

TARA YGLESIAS

Tara Yglesias has served as the deputy executive secretary of the Truman Foundation for the past three years and has been involved in the selection of Truman Scholars since 2001. During this time, she had the opportunity to study the trends and characteristics of each incoming class of Scholars. She used this knowledge to assist in the development of new Foundation programs and initiatives as well as the design of a new Foundation website and online application system. An attorney by training, she began her career by spending six years in the Office of the Public Defender in Fulton County, Georgia. She specialized in trial work and serious felonies and also assisted with the training of new attorneys. A former Truman Scholar from Pennsylvania, she also served as a Senior Scholar at Truman Scholars Leadership Week and the Foundation's Public Service Law Conference prior to joining the Foundation's staff.

One of the Truman Foundation's proudest accomplishments is our reputation for being accessible and transparent. We offer a wealth of information to faculty representatives and applicants via our website. We provide prompt and responsive answers to phone and e-mail inquiries, and give feedback on the written applications of those candidates not selected for interview. There are very few, if any, questions that we will not answer when it comes to our process and mission.

But with a full-time staff of six, a massive selection cycle, and the strikingly limited budget that can only be found at a government agency, there are a number of questions that we simply cannot answer to our satisfaction (or the satisfaction of our faculty reps). Every faculty rep's favorite unanswerable Truman question is likely our most difficult question to answer: "Why wasn't my [insert superlative] student selected?"

We can normally answer this question insofar as it relates to someone not selected for interview—we attend the entire reading panel and have written notes from each reader. But for those not selected at interview, we run into special problems. First, a Foundation staff member does not attend every interview. Since we cannot offer feedback on all interviews, we feel it would be unfair to offer feedback on some. Second, even if we did attend the interviews, we would still sometimes have difficultly articulating why one student was selected over another.

Often the distinction rests on a simple, but intangible, criteria: "Will this student be a good Truman Scholar? Will he or she add something to the Truman Scholar community?" Since most of our panelists are Truman Scholars, the answers to these questions are often based on their own experience with the Truman community.

Understanding this community (and the value placed on it by Scholars) is critical to appreciating both what causes a student to be selected as a Scholar as well as why it is important to have a wide variety of Scholars with a diversity of interests.

The Truman Community: More Than a Check

When the Foundation started in the late 1970s, Scholars were treated to a brief weekend in Missouri and a generous check. As the cost of education rose, the Foundation began to examine ways to add value to the program. Additional appropriation from Congress seemed unlikely, particularly in any amount that would change the award considerably. Instead the Foundation began to explore how to better develop the community of Scholars.

In the early 1990s, the Foundation implemented the first program to enhance the community of Truman Scholars: the Truman Scholars Leadership Week (TSLW). The program had a simple goal: bring Scholars together for a week to instill in them a sense of community and underscore the value of public service. The Foundation provides information on a variety of other competitive fellowships, public service career paths, and distinguished graduate schools. Scholars work together on group policy projects and community service projects. And lest we forget, there is a talent show at the end of the week—entirely produced by Scholars. But with so many different types of students with diverse backgrounds, interests, and goals, the Foundation was initially concerned about how TSLW could effectively build a community in such a short time.

As it turned out, building community was much easier than anyone anticipated. In spite of all of their differences, the Scholars came together almost immediately thanks to their shared values. There were few "dueling resumes," but instead numerous conversations on how to sustain a lifetime in public service. Self-promotion turned to roommate promotion ("He did this amazing fruit bat project in Costa Rica!"). Even the competition for class speaker—such as it was—turned into an adorable tug of war between two people who each thought the other would be the better speaker. To our surprise, Scholars from different social, political, economic, and educational backgrounds easily came together to form lasting relationships.

The Scholars also quickly developed relationships with the staff of the Foundation and the Senior Scholars, distinguished Truman Alumni who are invited to staff TSLW. Many Senior Scholars found future interns, staffers, and partners in advocacy from this group. One of our Senior Scholars, who had just been selected to edit the journal *Oxford International Review (OIR)* as part of a faculty appointment, was so inspired by the spirit of TSLW, she redefined the notion of a traditional academic journal. Instead of producing a scholarly journal and perhaps mentoring a few students along the way, she has decided to make mentoring students the main mission of *OIR*. The journal becomes a by-product of the mentoring relationship.

She has hired a number of Truman Scholars to work for her and provided them with opportunities they would not have had outside the Truman community. One Scholar went to North Korea as part of a research team. Another Scholar traveled to Iraq to interview government officials, many of whom are rarely interviewed by Western media. This type of public service—contributing to scholarly discourse through research and mentoring—might seem unusual for a program that was designed primarily to promote government service. But the goals of the journal and the opportunities afforded to students are a variety of service that is entirely in line with the values of our program.

The Truman Community: More Than a Week

Within a few years, the Foundation started Summer Institute (SI) as a way to continue the Truman community beyond TSLW. SI allows Scholars to come to Washington, DC, after they finish college to engage in a variety of Foundation programming as well as a ten-week internship with a government agency or non-profit.

Watching SI unfold is always fascinating. Although most of these students have no prior relationship other than spending a week in Missouri, they are immediately drawn to one another as old friends. Within a week, they have set up communal dinner parties, service activities, and Spanish language study groups. Even the occasional Scholar who attends SI with a different Scholar class is welcomed openly.

For many Scholars, SI is where the most interesting opportunities arise. Scholars with backgrounds in the hard sciences find themselves working with children—not numbers—for the first time ever. Students who were planning to go straight to graduate school are suddenly fielding job offers from their summer employers (and some are even more surprised to find that these employers might be willing to pay for graduate school).

As part of SI, we offer an odd little day called "Arts and Public Policy." This day grew out of our desire to challenge our Scholars' notions of public service. While many of our Scholars are individually talented in music or art, few see these talents as an avenue of public service. We worked with the Liz Lerman Dance Exchange to develop a program that explores dance as a medium of service and community building. The Scholars often begin the day uncomfortable and skeptical, but end with a newfound appreciation for art as a medium for service. Several of our students have continued working with the Dance Exchange even after this day is over. One recently started law school but is using her dance training to work with underprivileged girls. While this Scholar's dream is to be a juvenile court defense attorney, her new vision is one where children avoid becoming court involved because they have other creative outlets. This ability to capitalize upon the skills of individual Scholars to create new service opportunities is exactly what the Truman community hopes to achieve.

The Truman Community: Case Closed

The Truman Foundation commits significant time to surveying applicants, faculty reps, and Scholars. And we have discovered that nearly all of these groups agree that students are more likely to stick with a career in public service if they receive some sort of "inoculation" every now and again. This sentiment seemed to be especially true for those students involved in professions, such as the law, that often placed pressure on individuals not to enter into public service. The Public Service Law Conference (PSLC) was developed to counter this trend. PSLC is a weekend seminar designed to provide public service guidance to those students who might need it most. The conference discusses job hunting strategies, managing debt, and avoiding burnout.

Although the Scholars who attend this weekend come from many different Scholar years and might never have met before, the group is more cohesive than one would imagine possible for a group of would-be lawyers. Most of our guest speakers have a hard time believing that these Scholars do not all attend the same law school. In many ways, this community bonds quickly over shared experiences.

For many Scholars, the public service program at their law school is quite robust. But the allure of big firm dollars is quite seductive, especially for the top students in the class. One Scholar came to PSLC with just such a dilemma. She went to law school intending to work in politics when she graduated. She excelled at law school and found that her school was putting increased pressure on her to consider jobs at law firms. At the same time, she started volunteering for a local social services group that provided assistance to undocumented workers. Here, she said she found her true calling.

While at PSLC, she met a Senior Scholar who had connections with advocacy groups that work on behalf of undocumented workers. The Senior Scholar was able to put her in touch with someone who provided her an internship. Four years later, the Scholar is now an attorney with that same non-profit.

The Truman Community: Moving Forward

The Truman Fellows program has grown out of the same notion that providing a public service inoculation will allow students to stay on track with their goals. The Fellows program is designed to extend the experience of SI by allowing students to stay in DC for a full year. During this time, Scholars work in public service jobs (either with the government or non-profits), perform community service projects, and attend a variety of classes designed to provide professional development. The Truman Scholars Association, our alumni group, also provides each student with a mentor.

This past year, the Scholars took on a DC-area community center as a project. The community center project was an addition to their Fellows service projects. A number of the Scholars lived in a transitional neighborhood in DC. The Scholars felt that they should give back to the community that they were going to be a part of (albeit for only a short time). Together the Scholars wrote grant proposals, designed a website, published a newsletter, and helped refurbish the center.

We have also tried to provide a number of other opportunities for community outside our programs. First, we have developed a new Scholar website, listing additional opportunities for Scholars and providing a place where Scholars can look up other Scholars. Second, we are collaborating more closely with our alumni to provide additional inroads to graduate schools, jobs, and fellowships. Finally, we are working with other federal government agencies to ensure that those Scholars who do wish to join the federal service can do so with minimal difficulty. We currently have two direct hiring authorities as well as an exemption for our Scholars from the written exam for Foreign Service officers.

But Wait! Isn't There More?

Whenever we are asked for information about the Truman community and the opportunities that it provides, we are invariably asked for names of prominent Truman Scholars. We are proud to count among our distinguished alumni a state governor and numerous state executives. We can boast of several high-ranking government officials, judges, and state legislators. We even have a number of media personalities and a few veterans of reality TV. One of our Scholars writes romance novels when she is not serving in her state legislature. We are proud of every one of these Scholars.

But we do not wish to leave the impression that such public success is all we value. We also boast of a man who is the only ob-gyn for eight counties in the rural Midwest. We have Scholars who founded charter schools and work every day to ensure a better education for everyone. Some Scholars are serving in the armed forces, manning research laboratories, and working at the Federal Reserve Bank. We have professors and U.S. Attorneys and the occasional public defender. There are Truman Scholar engineers and chemists. These Scholars who often labor without public recognition are every bit as important to us as the big name Scholars we could mention.

We are pleased to have had a part in creating a community that would value all of these people equally. We are proud that our Scholars rarely let their egos get in the way of their service to others. And we are happy to welcome into the community all those who share the notion that public service is the highest value, regardless of whether a person wants to contribute through medicine, engineering, the law, art, or public policy. Mr. Truman would not have had it any other way.

11

Why Visit the United Kingdom
Confession of a Journeyman Fellowship Advisor

MARK BAUER

Mark Bauer, associate director of the Office of International Education and Fellowship Programs at Yale University, focuses his fellowship advising on the U.K. and Irish fellowships. He has taught at Yale since 1996—first for the English Language Institute, a summer program for advanced international students, and later for the English Department. He also serves as the writing tutor of one of Yale's residential colleges and is a member of the NAFA board.

Getting Started

I joined Yale's young office of International Education and Fellowship Programs in May of 2001 as a half-time fellowship advisor, charged with helping students prepare for U.K. and Irish fellowship competitions and with administering Yale's endorsement and/or selection process for these awards. As the writing tutor for one of our residential colleges, I had helped students with their fellowship essays for a number of years (though never with a Marshall or Rhodes essay). But I knew nothing about the education systems in the United Kingdom and Ireland, nothing of use about Oxford or Cambridge, or the federated colleges and institutes that comprise the University of London, let alone about universities such as Warwick, Edinburgh, or Trinity College, Dublin. Fortunately, that June, NAFA had its first national conference. I went to Tulsa as a veritable sponge for all things having to do with the Marshall, Mitchell, Rhodes, and the brand new Gates/Cambridge and came away with enough basic information to guide me and my students through that first fall fellowship season. I leaned mightily on faculty and deans who had administered and advised for these scholarships before me, and I shamelessly learned with my students as they researched various programs. When they asked questions that stumped me, I e-mailed Elliot Gerson or Terri Evans (the Boston Marshall officer at the time). When the dust cleared that first year, I knew I had cobbled together a patchwork understanding, and nothing more.

So it was with great excitement that I joined Betsy Vardaman and Ann Brown and Suzanne McCray and the rest of our team for NAFA's first site visit to the United Kingdom. Several things stand out from that first trip that have been particularly helpful to me as a fellowship advisor. Even our short time in London was enough to make it very clear what an extraordinary depth and range of academic and cultural resources the city itself makes available to our students. Without the opportunity to have visited the British Library, the British Museum, the National Gallery, and West-minster Abbey (on our first trip) and the Tate Modern, the Courtauld Institute, I would not be able to speak to my students about the holdings of these institutions and the excitement, rewards (and frustrations) of studying in a great city.

Specific Institutions and Resources

I learned that LSE, poised in the heart of the City, close to Bush House (home of the BBC) and the Inns of Court, like UCL and Kings, makes excellent use of London's resources, its media and government offices and officials, as well as the constant stream of visiting academics, business leaders, and other international policy officers; its array of taught master's programs draws on these resources and the strength of its faculty, but does so unevenly. In its effort to market a broad range of niche master's courses as a means of generating income for the school and its research programs, some courses are better conceived than others and provide better supervisions for their students. Our visits allowed me to do more than to encourage my students to carefully research the quality of the programs they are considering; the visits also gave me contact information for faculty in well-established programs, information that I pass on to my students to help them in their research.

Indeed, these contacts at each of the universities we visited have become an invaluable advising resource in themselves. Not only do I give students the names of pertinent contacts, I also e-mail from time to time people whom we met on our trips with questions about programs; and these e-mails in turn invariably introduce me to other faculty members who can be of assistance to my students.

On the subject of researching programs, our first trip also gave me a much better understanding of the Research Assessment Exercises (RAE),[1] how they can be used to encourage students to look beyond the golden triangle of Oxford, Cambridge, and LSE for strong programs in other universities. My students now know to look at 5 and 5* departments for programs that may interest them, but they also know that they need to look beyond these scores to investigate the particulars of various programs and faculty research interests. Our session at the British Council during our first visit also introduced us to other rankings, official and unofficial, from the Quality Assurance Assessments to the various League Tables.[2] Again this is information that I share with students now with a much better understanding of how these (largely undergraduate indices) can be helpful in providing suggestive information regarding taught masters courses.

Oxford and Cambridge were of course high on our agenda in both NAFA visits to U.K. universities. During the first trip to Oxford, I recall being particularly impressed with how difficult it is for U.S. students to be accepted to certain programs, especially international relations, economics, and philosophy. That Rhodes Scholars might not get into international relation (IR) was a real eye-opener and important for me to know, since this is such a high interest program. It was reassuring to learn that scholars who are not accepted into IR often get to work with some of the same faculty by undertaking an appropriate area study, development studies, or other related courses. At Cambridge, as well as hearing about particularly strong programs, we also got a much better idea of the interface between the new Gates scholarship and the university. Again, it has been invaluable to learn about the importance of the "endorsement" role of the Cambridge departments and how the timing of the process plays out, even after the Gates interviews.

Of course, one of the features that most distinguishes Oxford and Cambridge is the role of the colleges in instruction (for undergraduates) and in student life. It was one thing to know this in the abstract, but only a visit could make the diversity of college accommodations and character vividly concrete. I know that Gates Provost Gordon Johnson thinks too much can be made about the importance of college choice and that scholars can grow attached to and be happy with any college, but I think that such matters as distance from town center, proportion of graduates to undergrads, accommodations for people with disabilities, funds to subsidize meals, activities, and such, character of the Middle Common Room, and where the college ethos lies on a "High Table to Bolshy" continuum—all these are legitimate matters for a student to take into consideration. At a minimum, I would much rather students take some time to research their options and make informed choices than leave college choice blank on university applications. They are then much more likely to find a place in a college that fits well with their interests.

As well as visiting several London schools, Oxford, and Cambridge, our first trip took us to Durham, York, and two former polytechnics, Westminster and Oxford Brooks, as well as to Edinburgh and St. Andrews in Scotland. At these schools three things stand out for me that made visiting particularly worthwhile. The first has to do with being introduced to the particular specialties of these institutions. We are primed to expect excellence at London and Oxbridge, but it is very important to learn about the strengths that distinguish other schools. In some instances, we discovered programs that Oxbridge does not have or does not do well (Communication Studies at Westminster and its close relation with the BBC). In other cases we learned about particular resources and faculty concentrations that make these schools very attractive choices even in areas of strength at London or Oxbridge (history at Oxford Brooks, or English, especially Old Norse at Durham, or security studies at St. Andrews, for example).

The second feature of these schools that stands out for me as an advisor is that they may offer our students opportunities to immerse themselves more completely in an English or international environment.

London is, of course, a thoroughly cosmopolitan city, but it can also be uncharacteristic and a bit hard to settle into in the short space of a year or two. And at Cambridge and, even more, at Oxford being surrounded by Americans can be all too easy. Schools such as Durham, York, East Anglia, Essex, Warwick, and Birmingham all have strong programs that will attract U.S. students; they can also be particularly rewarding to students interested in getting to know English and other international students and getting outside of the "American bubble." Similar benefits also hold for students at Glasgow, St. Andrews, or Edinburgh.

The third reason visits to these schools have been particularly helpful to me as an advisor is that I now have a much better sense not just of the academic strengths of more schools but also of the very different character of these institutions and their environs. It helps to be able to talk about the urban energy and grittiness of a Westminster (or LSE for that matter) as compared to more suburban college environs of the old market and cathedral towns of York and Durham.[3] My students are fortunate in having quite a few people they can turn to when they want to find out about what it might be like for them to study at Oxbridge or the University of London; I serve as that resource for students who are considering less well known schools.

Because I had to leave the second U.K. tour before the visit to Manchester, I missed learning in detail about the newly combined university and its many strengths. (Even a cursory glance at the RAE for Manchester shows a sterling array of 5 and 5* scores.) The school that I learned the most about on our second trip was Warwick. Lead by an American (David VandeLinde), it has the most familiar structure and ethos for U.S. students as well as an outstanding academic record (Twenty-five out of Twenty-six departments are rated 5 or 5* on the 2001 RAE, and Warwick's reputation has only continued to grow). I do not hesitate to recommend that students look into programs at Warwick. It draws accomplished students from all over the world, has strong programs, and gets students outside of the Oxbridge/London triangle. Both Warwick and Manchester also have funding schemes to encourage top-flight North American students to take advantage of their graduate programs *(http://www.manchester.ac.uk/postgraduate/ funding/international/scholarships/; http://www2.warwick.ac.uk/services/ international/applying/scholarships/countryspecific/postgraduate/#nam).*[4]

Larger Lessons

While the faculty members (and other university officers) we met with during these visits kindly provided their contact information and encouraged us and our students to be in touch if we had questions, they also made it clear that inquiries (especially from students) should only come after they had carefully reviewed the information available online. Though happy to be of help, our university contacts could not undertake burdensome e-mail advising. Questions about particular courses or programs should usually be addressed to the heads of those courses (and not the teaching faculty); questions for faculty should usually be limited to their research interests or other substantive scholarly inquiries. Students applying for taught courses need not get in touch with faculty members to secure encouragement to apply; whereas students applying for research masters or doctorates should introduce themselves and their research interests to appropriate faculty and try to secure their support—especially for fellowships such as the Fulbright that require letters of affiliation.

One of the features of our first U.K. visit that made it so rewarding was the opportunity to talk with students at the various universities. Many of these students were on scholarships and could give us insight into the different scholarship competitions. Whether on scholarships or not, these students were extremely helpful in providing informal evaluations of the particular programs/courses they were pursuing. In planning our second trip, we tried to build more opportunities for talking with students into our visit. By staying in London at the Goodenough club, we shared the dining hall and college pub with the London Marshall and Fulbright scholars as well as with other students attending many of the University of London's schools and colleges.[5] We arranged an invaluable roundtable conversation with a group of Marshall Scholars based in London and at each of our subsequent university visits conferred with students about their academic, scholarship, residential, and other life experiences and the advice they would offer to students interested in study in the United Kingdom and Ireland.

Yes, hearing from faculty and program heads about the detail of their strong programs is exciting and gives me information I can pass on; but the candor and range of conversations possible with students about academic matters and other opportunities and experiences was for me particularly rewarding, and only possible by visiting the students where they are living and studying. Even at schools which have the benefit of attracting Gates, Marshall, Mitchell, or Rhodes Scholars to their graduate and professional schools, neither advisors nor our students have the opportunity to meet with such a comprehensive group of scholars engaged in such a wide range of disciplines and courses of study as we do on our NAFA visits.

From these conversations, I have learned how very helpful it is for our students to have direct contact with students who are studying (or who have recently studied) in the programs that they are considering. It is invaluable for us, and for them, to hear firsthand about the uneven quality of various programs, about the unsuspected differences and difficulties that study in a new culture (even one so seemingly similar) entails, and of course about the extraordinary opportunities (for research and scholarship, travel and fellowship) that "schemes" such as the Fulbright, Gates, Marshall, Mitchell, and Rhodes provide.

That said, our trips to the United Kingdom and Ireland have made it clear that students are sometimes too close to the experience or too idiosyncratic in their evaluations to provide authoritative guidance. That is why meeting and talking with many students is so important. I can and do encourage my students to contact people currently studying in programs they are interested in (and to seek out more than one student opinion). But, thanks to the conversations I've had with students in the United Kingdom, I can now temper and qualify some of the advice they might receive. And I can do this with some credibility.

As well as enabling me to become more knowledgeable about U.K. scholarships and opportunities in relatively short order, I'd say the greatest benefit that I have gained as an advisor from having participated in two sets of site visits to U.K. institutions is that sense of assurance that comes from having gained considerable (albeit indirect) experience with U.K. institutions, faculty, scholars, scholarships, and environs. A very considerable side benefit, of course, is that these trips have introduced me to a set of wonderful NAFA advisors who have also become good friends. There is nothing like being on a bus trip from college to college (or helping to plan such a trip) for bringing out peoples' senses of humor, their resourcefulness, and capacity for making the most of long hours. As well as the invaluable NAFA listserv, I now have a group of advisor friends whom I can call or e-mail when questions arise about students' situations or other conundrums.

I feel confident that in this I can speak for all of us who have benefited from participating in one of NAFA's study trips to the United Kingdom. They have helped me become much better informed and more confident than I could have imagined being when I started this job, and they have given me the support, good advice, and counsel of a wonderful circle of fellowship advisor friends. I know that British higher education is changing in some fundamental ways with the consolidation or elimination of some programs, with the continuing development of new, interdisciplinary master's and even doctoral programs, with changes in governance and research funding that can quickly trickle down to affect courses—and I know that, in order to have a better handle on these and other changes, I will want to be a participant when NAFA next leads a study trip to universities in the United Kingdom. My students and colleagues have come to expect someone who has a certain "mastery" in this field, and participation in NAFA study trips helps me meet these expectations.

12

Why Ireland?

JANE MORRIS

*Jane Morris is a 1978 graduate of Villanova University with both a B.S. in
Biology and a B.A. in Honors. After receiving an M.A. in Biology from
Bryn Mawr College, Jane worked as a research scientist in both the private
and public sector for nearly twenty years. In September 2001, she became
Villanova's first director of Competitive Grants and Awards. In this capacity,
Ms. Morris provides guidance for students applying for nationally competitive
scholarships and direction for the Connelly Delouvrier International Scholars
Program, the Presidential Scholarship Program, and the Villanova
University Undergraduate Student Collaborative Research Awards. In
addition, Ms. Morris currently serves as secretary for NAFA. In 2004 and
2006, she directed site visits by NAFA members to universities in the United
Kingdom, Ireland, and Northern Ireland.*

Ireland—specifically, Northern Ireland—is the land of my ancestors. In
the late nineteenth century my Coyle/McGlinchey family left their
home in search of new opportunities in America. Obviously, this is a common story; in the 2000 U.S. census, nearly thirty-four million Americans

claimed Irish ancestry. In the mid-1990s, Ireland experienced a period of rapid economic growth commonly referred to as the "Celtic Tiger." In the wake of this prosperity, Ireland gained a newfound status as one of Europe's wealthier countries. Transnational corporations such as Dell, Intel, Microsoft, and Google connect the United States to the rest of Europe through their headquarters in Ireland. The ties that bind the United States and Ireland are deep, and in the last decade they have grown stronger through the efforts of the U.S.-Ireland Alliance and the George J. Mitchell Scholarship. NAFA traces its own roots to this same time period and, in a way, NAFA and the Mitchell Scholarship Program have grown alongside each other. It was only natural that as NAFA planned site visits to universities in the United Kingdom, we would expand our sites to include Ireland.

After a highly successful NAFA tour of higher education in England and Scotland in 2002, Dell Pendergrast, then the Mitchell scholarship director, suggested Ireland as a location for a subsequent NAFA trip. NAFANs, eager to find new opportunities for postgraduate studies and funding for their students, were excited at the prospect of learning more about Irish universities and their offerings for American students. I had the honor of leading a group of twenty-five NAFA members on a whirlwind tour of six universities in Northern Ireland and the Republic of Ireland in the summer of 2004. In the North, we visited Queen's University Belfast and the University of Ulster. We then traveled to Dublin and toured Trinity College Dublin, University College Dublin, and Dublin City University. We trekked across the country to Galway where we toured the National University of Ireland Galway. Along the way, we also met representatives from the University of Limerick and University College Maynooth. One of the things that we learned through this experience was Ireland's unique and fortunate situation with respect to scholarships for American students. Since Northern Ireland is part of the United Kingdom, American students can apply not only for a Mitchell Scholarship, but they are also eligible for the Marshall to study at Queen's or Ulster. Ireland also has a vibrant Fulbright program open for study at all Irish universities.

At each of the schools we visited, we toured beautiful campuses, witnessed the results of growth and expansion of both physical structures as well as interdisciplinary curricula, and were generally treated with characteristic warmth and grace by each and every Irish university representative with whom we met. We also had the opportunity to hear from American postgraduate students at each of the schools we toured. Current U.S. students enrolled in Irish institutions were able to provide us with firsthand accounts of their experiences with higher education in Ireland. Most of the students found the transition from the American system of teacher-driven education to the more independent style of learning in Ireland somewhat frustrating at first. This was an important piece of information for NAFA advisers to pass along to their students who hoped to study in Ireland.

An attractive feature of postgraduate study in Ireland for American students is the opportunity to complete a one-year taught master's degree and a Ph.D. in three–four years rather than the four–six that is more typical in the United States. American students are also appreciative of the interdisciplinary programs found at Irish universities. Many of the students with whom we met were not funded through Mitchell, Marshall, or Fulbright. Some students—particularly those pursuing Ph.D. studies—were able to find support through the universities where they were studying; most, however, had American financial aid in the form of loans and grants. All agreed that they loved Ireland.

At the University of Ulster, we were greeted by the pro-vice chancellor for Teaching and Learning and we learned that the University of Ulster, the largest university on the island of Ireland, was founded by Royal Charter in 1984 but has roots dating back 150 years. Over 28,000 students attend the university, which has four campuses in Belfast, Coleraine, Jordanstowne, and Magee. We then heard presentations from representatives from the faculties of Arts, Social Sciences, Life and Health Sciences, Engineering, and Business and Management. The university is home to many exciting and internationally recognized programs, but we were all very impressed with INCORE, the International Centre of Excellence for Peace and Conflict Studies. Many of us were wishing that we could participate in this innovative program that addresses the causes and consequences of conflict, not only in Northern Ireland, but internationally as well. After lunch hosted graciously by President Gerry McKenna, we were off to tour the natural beauty of the Northern Ireland coastline.

After hearing for so many years about tensions and conflict in the neighborhoods of Belfast, we were delighted to find a growing and prosperous city. Queen's University Belfast welcomed us to their beautiful campus near the heart of the city. We listened attentively to presentations from faculty representatives about their course offerings and research centers. Of note at Queen's are the Sonic Arts Research Centre, an interdisciplinary research program in music technology, and the Seamus Heaney Centre for Poetry. After an informative meeting with U.S. graduate students and lunch with University staff in the Great Hall, we were treated to a profoundly moving tour of Catholic and Protestant neighborhoods in Belfast guided by Dominic Bryan, the Director of the Institute of Irish Studies at Queen's. There, we viewed protective fences and walls as well as massive murals of remembrance containing declarations of resolve, resistance, and demands. As my Villanova colleague, Edwin Goff, noted in his post-trip reflections, the experience was "deeply unsettling, but beautiful nevertheless." We left Belfast with a new perspective on a city with a long and painful history that has resurrected to become a thriving intellectual and cultural center to which our students would certainly be attracted.

If it's Wednesday, it must be Dublin—with two universities to visit on one day. Early in the day we were off to historic Trinity College Dublin and a morning filled with hospitality and information. We met with the faculty deans who introduced us to the five university faculties. We learned about several remarkable programs within each of these faculties including International Integrations Studies, Irish Theatre and Film Studies, and Ecumenics from the presentation on the Arts, Humanities, and Social Sciences Faculties as well as Physics, Molecular Medicine, and Music and Media Technologies from Science, Health Sciences, and Engineering. Many of these programs, such as Ecumenics and Music and Media Technologies, follow an interdisciplinary approach to learning and research. After our coffee with American students, the college librarian treated us to a tour of the Old Library and a private viewing of the Book of Kells.

In the afternoon, we proceeded on to University College Dublin where we were met by Associate Registrar Rodney Thom and Marie Lawlor, manager of the International Office, who took us on a tour of this expansive and beautiful campus. During a presentation on UCD postgraduate programs we were impressed by the strength of the UCD research centers and the focus on interdisciplinary learning. Programs such as the Humanities Institute of Ireland and the Conway Institute of Biomolecular and Biomedical Research and the existence of a separate faculty of Interdisciplinary Studies illustrate UCD's commitment to research at the highest level across disciplines. Our day culminated in a lovely reception at the University Industry Center where we were able to meet informally with academics, administrators, and students. Among the invited guests were Carmel Coyle, executive director of the Fulbright Commission in Dublin, and Dr. David Redmond, registrar from the National University of Ireland Maynooth. At the end of the day, we were tired but invigorated by all that we had learned.

Dublin City University was our next stop. We were greeted warmly by Dean of International Studies, Dr. Claire Bohan. As we walked across the campus to our meeting venue, we were all struck by the vast amount of on-going construction and building renovation. It was obvious to all that DCU was in a phase of remarkable growth, and a significant investment in higher education was in process. During our meeting with representatives from faculties and research centers as well as with Carmel Lawlor, coordinator of International Information, we were once again struck with the degree of cross-disciplinary programs such as LInK, the Learning, Innovation and Knowledge Research Centre.

On our way to a sumptuous lunch, we had an official tour of this young university, including the Helix, a dazzling performing arts center whose stunning architecture contains several venues allowing for a wide range of performances and cultural presentations. At lunch, I had the honor of dining with a number of professors and with Mr. Patrick McDermott, chief executive officer of the DCU Educational Trust, which supports the growth and development of the university. The Helix was among the projects funded through the Trust, which also engages in significant community outreach through its scholarship programs for economically disadvantaged students. DCU was yet another example of Ireland's commitment to higher education and the subsequent enhancement of the broader, civil community.

Sad to leave Dublin, we climbed on the bus and drove across breathtaking natural beauty to the west coast of Ireland and the city of Galway, the site of our final university visit. The National University of Ireland Galway was founded in 1845 and, like the other universities we visited, it has grown tremendously in recent years. Professor Jim Browne officially welcomed us, and Michael Kavanagh, assistant secretary in the Registrar's Office, gave us an overview of the university. We then learned more about NUI Galway's extensive research programs and we were once again struck by a fierce commitment to cross-disciplinary exploration. This theme continued in the presentations from the deans of six of the seven university faculties. From taught master's programs to Ph.D. research, NUI Galway is yet another Irish university to which American students would be—and are—drawn. On our tour of this beautiful campus situated on the River Corrib, we passed both older, ivy-covered stone buildings and glistening new facilities dedicated to learning and research at the highest level. We were also struck by the strong presence of the Irish language throughout. Our experiences of higher education in Ireland exemplified for us the country's pride in their deep and often painful history and their commitment to the future, investing mightily in higher education along the way. As we came to the end of our 2004 tour of Irish universities, we gathered together with our Galway hosts at the Glenlo Abbey Hotel for a splendid evening of dining, conversation, gratitude, and delight in all that we learned and in the new relationships that we forged with our colleagues in Ireland. We were anxious to bring all of this information to our students at home and we hoped fervently that we would soon have an opportunity to return to this beautiful country steeped in history and exploding in modernity.

The next opportunity for NAFA to return to Ireland arose from discussions of a proposed international symposium on higher education in the United Kingdom. This time, we planned to forego site visits as we had done in our previous trips and we proposed to have the U.K. universities travel to Cambridge to meet with NAFA representatives. In this new format, we wove discussions of issues of international educational exchange pertinent to both the U.K. and U.S. schools into discussions of academic programs and research opportunities at the U.K. institutions. Given what we had discovered about higher education in Ireland during our 2004 tour, we decided to continue our conversations in Dublin, inviting all nine Irish universities to meet for a day-long conference at University College Dublin. Marie Lawlor, whom we had met in 2004, undertook the herculean task of arranging an array of speakers that included institutional representatives from the universities, students, and leaders from various agencies of higher education in Ireland. We even had a visit from the U.S. ambassador to Ireland, James Kenny, who emphasized for us the strength of the Irish economy and Ireland's passion for supporting education, especially at the highest levels. There were several recurring themes that were reflective of our earlier visit. Primary among these themes was the Irish government's intention to make education, particularly the third and fourth levels (postgraduate/Ph.D.), a high priority by committing a substantial portion of its budget to insure that Irish higher education will be competitive in an increasingly global market. With an emphasis on supporting research efforts, the goals for this investment are to make Irish universities distinctive while encouraging inter-institutional collaboration both among the Irish universities and internationally. Interdisciplinary research and learning, particularly in technology and science, continue to thrive in Irish schools.

Our day began in beautiful O'Reilly Hall at UCD with traditional Irish hospitality and abundant coffee, tea and danish. Dr. Philip Nolan, UCD registrar and vice president for Academic Affairs, opened the symposium with an overview on recent changes in Irish universities. Emphasizing Ireland's need for global competitiveness, Dr. Nolan outlined the government's budgetary commitment to postgraduate education and the various agencies responsible for oversight of those funds. The Programme for Research at Third-Level Institutions (PRLTI, *http://www.hea.ie/PRLTI/*) received €650 million to fund research institutes such as UCD's Conway Institute of Biomolecular and Biomedical Research and Humanities Institute of Ireland. Science Foundation Ireland (SFI) supports research in the sciences, engineering, and technology through a €600 million allotment of funds, while the Strategy for Science, Technology and Innovation 2006–2013 has €3.8 billion to support infrastructure and programs aimed at doubling the number of Ph.D. graduates by 2013. The Strategic Innovation Fund (SIF) will use €300 million to reform third level (postgraduate, master's-level) and build a fourth level (Ph.D.-level). Other agencies with increased funding are the Irish Research Council for Humanities and Social Sciences (IRCHSS), the Irish Research Council for Science, Engineering and Technology (IRCSET), and the Health Research Board (HRB). In addition to the establishment of research institutes and centers of excellence, another goal of this funding blitzkrieg is to restructure graduate education to bring Irish higher education more closely aligned with the Bologna Process, a plan to bring standardized academics and quality assurance practices throughout European higher education (*http://ec.europa.eu/education/policies/educ/ bologna/bologna_en.html*).

Dr. Padraig Walsh, the chief executive of the Irish Universities Quality Board (IUQB), reviewed the process of quality assurance among the Irish universities. Regulated by the Universities Act of 1997, the IUQB was established in 2003 and is responsible for the external quality assurance (QA) process in the Irish universities. In a country with a long tradition of autonomy for Irish universities, the quality assurance process has led to a balance of accountability and autonomy. Each Irish university is responsible for evaluating each department, faculty, and service provided by the university. The IUQB organizes external QA in the universities while the Higher Education Authority (HEA) coordinates external QA of the university sector. Each university must publish the outcome of evaluations and must implement recommendations made. Reports of evaluations can be found on university websites as well as the IUQB website (*http:// www.iuqb.ie*). In 2004, all seven Irish universities were reviewed by the European University Association (EUA) using reviewers from Europe and North America. This institutional evaluation mirrors the regional accrediting process in the U.S. The report is available on the IUQB website.

Dr. Eucharia Meehan, head of Research Programmes for the HEA, presented information on Irish education and the research system. Dr. Meehan documented thoroughly the impact of the "Celtic Tiger" on budgetary allocations for higher education and research support in Ireland. HEA research funding provides and enhances the infrastructure and capabilities for research, supports and enables strategic development and collaboration, and enhances the quality of research, education, and training. Of the allocations for research, forty-eight percent are dedicated to biosciences and biomedicine while technology, the environment, social sciences, humanities, and library resources comprise the remaining budget allocations. Through HEA funding, twenty-four of thirty-three research centers have been completed, state of the art equipment and 97,000 square meters research space have been provided, direct funding for 1,600 researchers (more then twenty-five percent from outside Ireland) has been awarded, and facilities for 1,200 postgrad students have been secured through investments. The HEA website (*www.hea.ie*) contains abundant information on Irish higher education and the recent advances in fostering and enabling a strong third and fourth level higher education system.

What does all of this mean for individual universities? Professor Michael Ryan, dean of Doctoral Studies and Post Doctoral Training at UCD, discussed the impact that these initiatives have had at UCD with respect to postgraduate education, specifically delivering the fourth level.

After an extensive review and consultation process, several changes were implemented; among these changes were efforts to recruit and support graduate students, introduce "modularisaton" of all taught master's programs, provide incentives for supervisors, and restructure Ph.D. programs. UCD has 226 taught postgraduate programs with 1,500 taught postgraduate modules available. In developing a structured Ph.D. program, UCD initiated a taught portion of the program to provide requisite skills for research and teaching while devoting the remainder of the program to supervised research. These changes have been adopted in line with Bologna Principles to continue UCD's aim of driving Ireland's knowledge, economy, and society.

The Irish Universities Association (IUA, *http://www.iua.ie*) is a representative body of the seven Irish universities that seeks to advance university education and research through the formulation and pursuit of collective policies and actions on behalf of the Irish universities. Conor O'Carroll, the assistant director for research of the IUA, outlined the various ways that the IUA influences and supports research policy in Ireland. The IUA works with government funding agencies such as Atlantic Philanthropies to enact the National Development Plan creating collaborative research institutes and attracting researchers from abroad. IUA operates the Marie Curie Office, the Researchers Mobility Portal, and *expertiseireland. com* to support researchers in Ireland. The Marie Curie Office is part of an international fellowship program that has attracted more than 250 high quality researchers from around the world to Ireland making Ireland the most successful European country in this program. The Researchers Mobility Portal (*http://www.researchcareersireland.com*) provides nuts and bolts support and advisory services to researchers coming to and leaving from Ireland. Expertiseireland (*http://www.expertiseireland.com*) is a research database for all of the Irish universities, the seven in the Republic and two in the North, containing updated profiles of nearly 3,500 researchers on the island of Ireland.

Our tours of higher education in Ireland have taken place both through university site visits and through conference participation. Each format has both pros and cons with respect to learning about Irish university programs and policies. Site visits provide an *in situ* view of the university and allow for meeting administrators, teachers, and students. The downside of site visits is the exhaustion of the travelers. The conference format certainly avoids the fatigue and allows for discussion of common issues. Both experiences have provided a wealth of information to NAFA advisors in preparing students to apply for the Mitchell, Fulbright, and Marshall Scholarships. More importantly, we have learned about Ireland's passionate commitment to postgraduate education, which they have backed commendably with abundant financial resources. Ireland is a country that recognizes the importance of research and education in securing economic security and growth and this can only mean wonderful things for Ireland and for students in the United States and around the world who wish to study in Ireland.

13

Coin of the Realm
Graduate Education in Britain

ELIZABETH VARDAMAN

Elizabeth Vardaman, associate dean in the College of Arts and Sciences and associate director of the Honors Program at Baylor University, Waco, Texas, has taught at Baylor since 1980. An exchange professor in China and assistant director for several Baylor abroad programs in England and The Netherlands, she has traveled extensively on behalf of the university and led the first NAFA tour of British higher education. Her overview of that trip, "Keys to the United Kingdom," was published in Beyond Winning. *She has been serving as a scholarship advisor since 1998 and was a charter member of the National Association of Fellowships Advisors. She and Jane Morris (Villanova University) co-chaired the 2006 NAFA Higher Education Symposia, in the United Kingdom and the Republic of Ireland.*

The National Association of Fellowships Advisors (NAFA)—In collaboration with Wolfson College, Cambridge University, The Gates Cambridge Trust, and The Marshall Commission—participated in a symposium on higher education, June 26–June 30, 2006, at Wolfson College. Representatives from thirty-five American colleges and universities[1] heard presentations by and engaged in conversations with representatives from international funding and educational agencies as well as directors of key programs at many British colleges, institutes, and universities.[2]

Broadly, the theme of the symposium was both the value of international educational exchange and the roles of scholarship students and scholarship advising in maximizing such exchange. To those ends, graduate opportunities and research programs across many disciplines at wide-ranging British academic institutions were explored. In response, NAFA provided materials and panel discussions to increase understanding of the American universities' perspectives. Through dialogue among all present, clearer insights into higher education issues in both the British and American spheres were achieved. Such experience enables NAFA to serve more effectively students who wish to apply for British graduate programs and to communicate to the organization's approximately 300 colleges and universities new insights and enhanced understanding of the extensive graduate school opportunities in Britain.

NAFA has organized two summer programs (2002 and 2004) where the participants traveled from university to university in England, Scotland, Northern Ireland, and the Republic of Ireland for visits to a rich array of institutions; those interactions with British and Irish educators were informative, even exhilarating. Buoyed by the higher education expertise and generous support from Dr. Gordon Johnson, president of Wolfson College, Cambridge, and provost of the Gates Cambridge, the 2006 planning committee decided to organize its first four days of the symposium in the United Kingdom at Cambridge and invite a variety of institutions to attend, with a day at Oxford University to follow.[3] Since representatives from programs at twelve institutions of higher learning in England and Wales, student scholars, and directors of the Gates, Fulbright U.K., and Marshall foundations made presentations to us, and we in turn engaged them in formal and informal settings at Wolfson, our days were very full. Combining these experiences with presentations at Oxford gave us much to consider and to share with NAFA and our students upon our return stateside.

Insights into Twelve British Institutions of Higher Learning

The following highlights focus on graduate education and are cobbled together from many resources, most of them provided at the Cambridge symposium: commentary, handouts, and presentations by U.K. university staff and faculty members; notes taken by NAFA members; supplemental information on university websites; university publications; British Council newsletters; and other recent higher education publications.[4] Further details from the universities' presentations are available on the NAFA website.

University of Cambridge

- Nearing its eight-hundredth anniversary (in 2009), yet fully engaged in Twenty-first century
- 17,500 students enroll, with about 7,500 of them graduate students (out of 11,500 graduate applicants)
- 2006–07 *Times Higher Education Supplement (THES)* has Cambridge ranked as number two in the world (Harvard took first place)
- Cambridge is number one in science, biomedicine, the arts and humanities, according to the *THES*, Cambridge. *See http://www.thes.co.uk/ worldrankings/*
- New Institute for Stem Cell Biology will be crucial part of the Cambridge Stem Cell Initiative

Understanding the Process of Application to Cambridge and to the Gates

- The University consists of six schools and thirty-one colleges. All of the faculties (in the United Kingdom sense of the word; that is to say, "departments" in American terminology) are grouped into one or the other of the six schools. The six schools are organized on a subject basis; each school covers research, teaching, graduate, and undergraduate work within its subject areas.[5]
- The Board of Graduate Studies, not the colleges, admits graduate students and acts as the overseer and administrative control of graduate studies across the university.[6] All the formal correspondence between a student and Cambridge is with this board—from initial application through to the award of the degree.
- The administrative side is handled by the Board of Graduate Studies, but students should look at the individual faculties (departments) and schools to see what is on offer.

- Substantive, good advice comes from departments: The Degree Committees make the decisions about admissions (as well as later about supervision, progress, and success of graduate students) and then forward those as recommendations to the Board of Graduate Studies for implementation.[7]
- Students need to understand who are the key professors, et cetera in their proposed area of study; there is no reason why they should not engage in correspondence directly with them, asking about research opportunities or the nature of courses, et cetera. A number of applicants do, though it is not always necessary, if for example, the student is applying for a straightforward taught master's course. It is very advisable if a student wants to do a Ph.D. because there might be particular professors or lab/archive/ library resources in Cambridge that are essential to the student's research.
- **The Gates Process:** This process was simplified in 2006. Students need to fill in fully the Cambridge Application Form, and if they go on to complete the sections that ask if they want to be considered for funding—that is to say, The Gates, et cetera—then copies of the application forms are automatically passed to the Trust. No separate application is needed; but the students will need to fill out the whole application form in full, and do their Gates essay, and have the additional reference.
- **Point of Clarification:** Two references are required for admission to Cambridge; these should be straight academic references. The additional reference for the Gates does not need to be limited solely to academic referents.

Cardiff University
- Number one in Civil Engineering, in City and Regional Planning, and in Psychology in the United Kingdom
- Four additional disciplines, for a total of seven, have Research Assessment Exercise (RAE) 5* ratings: Education, Optometry, English, and Religion[8]
- Research Priorities: Engineering, pharmaceuticals, nano-materials, biotechnology, bio-medical science, bio-informatics, and super-computing

- Recent Postgraduate Programs: Master's degrees in tissue engineering, lean operations, public administration, building energy, bio-photonics (the interface between laser optics, cell biology, and medicine), and data-information fusion
- Particular strengths in professional subjects: law, business, medicine, and architecture

Courtauld Institute of Art

- The only History of Art department to have been awarded the highest rating of 5* in the 2001 RAE assessment.
- Master's degrees are central focus of the program, with hundred students enrolled.[9]
- Each professor has eight students.
- Students interact with and become curators, critics, and artists. They do not necessarily have background in art history (for example: conservation and technology master's degree necessitates a science background). But they must have considerable self-motivation.
- "The Ph.D. program equips scholars with the discipline and training to produce substantial and sustained pieces of research and all the skills academic work entails."[10]

Imperial College, University of London

- Embodies and delivers scholarship, education, and research in science, engineering, and medicine with particular regard to their application in industry, commerce, and health care
- Ranked number nine in the world in the *Times Higher Education Supplement, 2006.* Ranked number one in Europe for technology studies
- 4,200 graduate students enrolled. Majority of Ph.D. students have master's degrees before they start
- Interdisciplinary emphasis. For example, in biomedical/environment/energy research, with new institutes that complement these areas
- Good business school with heavy emphasis on science /technology/entrepreneurialism

- Themes for study include defense and security, energy, health care, creating fuels, controlling allergies, obesity, public health, mathematical modeling of epidemics, stem cell research, and robotic surgery. (No humanities departments.)

Institute of Development Studies (IDS) at University of Sussex

- Integrates social sciences (economics, politics, sociology, and anthropology) to develop practical strategies for addressing world poverty
- United Kingdom has more than 120 development studies programs at postgraduate level (at LSE, Manchester, SOAS, Swansea in Wales, East Anglia, Reading, Leeds Birmingham, etc.)
- At IDS, key areas of research include (1) globalization, (2) governance, (3) how science and technology can improve the livelihood of the poor and promote social justice, (4) how and where citizen participation can affect social justice and development, and (5) understanding vulnerability and designing means of addressing it.
- A portfolio of M.A. programs, a two-year M.Phil., and one D.Phil. by research[11]
- Students need three to five years of field work.
- IDS "aims to challenge convention and to generate fresh ideas that foster new approaches to development policy and practice. Such problem-focused thinking requires a commitment to multidisciplinarity, not just within social sciences, but across research, teaching, and communications."[12]

London School of Economics and Political Science

- 3,000 at master's and 1,100 at Ph.D. level (one-half of total enrollments)
- Focuses teaching/research on knowledge and action in "real world" issues. Has links with employers around the world. 75,000 alumni, including heads of state
- RAE rankings of 5* in accounting and finance, anthropology, economics, law, philosophy, and social policy. The 2001 U.K. RAE rated LSE second among approximate 200 universities and colleges in England, with ninety-seven percent of its staff assessed

- The RAE 5** rating for international history. Sixty percent of the 100 graduate students in this area are Americans. The combination of high-tech aspects and lots of interaction with international faculty members creates a very popular course of study. Students receive extensive feedback on written work. This is a career-enhancing degree.
- LSE ranked seventeenth in the world by the *THES 2006–07.*
- Social sciences are regarded as second to Harvard University worldwide.

London School of Hygiene and Tropical Medicine, University of London

- Focus on informing policy and practice in national and international public health and tropical medicine
- Postgraduate only. Research and teaching units available. Students may move across three departments: (1) epidemiology and population health, (2) infectious and tropical diseases, and (3) public health and policy
- Research units include: Centers for Population Studies, Epidemiology, Medical Statistics, Immunology, and Public and Environmental Health
- Recent research: study showing safety of MMR (measles) vaccine, project revealing data from British American Tobacco's document archive, impact of intermittent treatment for malaria in children, and impact of pneumococcal vaccine trials in Gambia

Newcastle University

- Over 3,100 full-time graduate students of 18,000 students.
- 5* programs in the 2001 RAE in Music, Clinical Laboratory Studies, Nanotechnology, Film and Media Studies, Medicine, Biological Sciences, and Psychology
- Doctoral research areas include (1) Faculty of Humanities and Social Sciences, (2) Faculty of Medical Sciences, and (3) Faculty of Science, Agriculture & Engineering.
- MA and Diploma in Museum Studies
- An important national project—Premia—is housed at Newcastle for support of disabled research students. (*http://www.ncl.ac.uk/disability. services/postgradresearch/*).

- Newcastle has a new University Code of Practice for Research programs that mirrors the national concern in the United Kingdom for improving doctoral training in many areas.[13]

Peace Studies at University of Bradford

- MA in Peace Studies/International Politics and Security/Conflict Resolution—all are research driven. New MS in African Peace and Conflict.
- Largest academic center exclusively for study of peace and conflict anywhere in the world.
- Rotary World Peace Scholarship administered here.
- Conflict Resolution is an academic degree, not a practical training program.
- Includes research themes that are multidisciplinary, such as Peace-building in Societies Torn by Violence and Armed Conflict, Transitions toward Democracy, Conflict Studies, Conflict Resolution, and Area Studies in virtually every region of the world.[14]
- One hundred or more in MA program, average age twenty-four to twenty-five. Nonstandard applicants are welcome.

School of Oriental and African Studies (SOAS), University of London

- Brings together the largest aggregation of expertise in Middle Eastern and Islamic Studies in the United Kingdom.[15] Thirty full-time staff and as many as twenty additional staff with Islamic expertise scattered through other departments.
- Many conferences and seminars happen each week at SOAS, creating a lively campus. Thus, SOAS brings the regions to the disciplines, not just the other way round, and creates perspectives beyond Eurocentrism.
- History at SOAS earned one of only three 5*** ratings in Britain.
- Programs: Finance and Administration (for Asia and Africa governance); Economics (political economics with focus on disentangling conflicting laws); Anthropology; Art and Archaeology (strong presence in East Asian, Middle Eastern, African, and Islamic Art); Religious Studies (Middle-Eastern

religions, Christianity, Jewish Studies); Gender Studies; Music (small but beautifully formed department focused on ethnomusicology); Media and Film (non-Western film studies); Linguistics (first such U.K. department and home of the endangered language archive); and Language and Literature (from A to Zulu).[16]

University College London

- Addressing the world's most pressing environmental, health care, and communication challenges[17]
- Fifty eight departments received top ratings of 5 or 5* in 2001 RAE. Of these, fifteen departments have been classified by the Higher Education Funding council for England as Best 5*
- Ranked twenty-fifth in the world by *Times Higher Education Supplement, 2006–07*
- 7,000 graduate students
- Highlights: Stem Cell Research (into spinal cord repair), Biomedical Research, Cognitive Neuroscience (brain and mind sciences), London Center for Nanotechnology, Institute of Global Law, and Visual Development Unit (testing how children use the eye-brain functions normally and why this development may go wrong)

University of Manchester

- Largest university in the United Kingdom, with 35,500 students
- Top 5 or 5* in thirty-seven of forty-six subjects in the 2001 RAE assessment
- Four broad areas of education: Humanities, Engineering/Physical Sciences, Medical and Human Science, and Life Science
- Top career service program in the United Kingdom
- Interdisciplinary teaching in master's programs in Bio-Health Informatics; History of Science, Technology, and Medicine; Applied Theatre; Human Rights; Religion and Political Life; and Management of Science, Technology, and Innovation. Linguistics has a Chinese Studies division
- Interdisciplinary studies, such as Brooks World Poverty Institute, Manchester Interdisciplinary Biocentre, and Center for Interdisciplinary Research in the Arts

- Ranked fortieth in the world by *Times Higher Education Supplement,* (2006-2007)
- Specialist master's in many areas at Manchester Business School, including an MBA for people in the public sector.

Assessments and Changes in U.K. Doctoral Studies

Traditionally, the doctor of philosophy degree program in America has included both taught courses and academic research that leads to a dissertation. Nearly sixty years after its established formula was set in the United States (circa 1860), the doctorate was introduced at Oxford in 1917 with the intention that it would prepare students for an academic career. Much has changed about the uses of the doctorate in both the United States and in the United Kingdom in the past ninety years, and funding programs and think-tanks "on both sides of the pond" have been re-evaluating the process (focused on developing the researcher), the product (a dissertation), and the tensions produced between these two as they impact doctoral studies.[18]

Currently nearly two-thirds of the U.K. doctoral graduates do not enter academia; for those, employers want readiness to begin work and quick transition out of the academy and into commercial or "real world" issues.[19] Even for those staying in academe, the skills needed for successful academic careers are also changing.[20] Recognizing these concerns, the Higher Education Funding Council for England (HEFCE), together with the Research Councils and industry leaders, has launched a program of skills training and allocated funds for the implementation of these good practices.

Presenters at almost every session of our symposium made reference to this initiative (called the "Roberts Review"). Indeed, Professor Ella Ritchie from Newcastle University focused the majority of her remarks on this "changing national context" for higher education. She listed core competencies that an effective educational process should provide to a Ph.D. candidate, no matter the subject area or the intended career field after graduation. The list includes the capacity for original thought, the ability to identify and consider moral questions, and the ability to design well-organized communication. Additionally, all scholars should be able to deal with large quantities of complex information, as well as make connections across disciplines. Dr. Chris Park, author of "Redefining the Doctorate," adds another core competency to that list: the "ability to see oneself as a scholar-citizen who will connect his or her expertise to the needs of society."[21]

The Roberts Review created a list of skills that research students should have, and HEFCE required that institutions demonstrate how they were fulfilling the Roberts agenda. The list of skills offers graduate students an attractive array of improved support in the following areas: (1) research skills and techniques, (2) the research environment, (3) research management, (4) personal effectiveness, (5) communication skills, (6) networking and team working, and (7) career management.[22] Dr. Ritchie provided us with detailed analysis of how Newcastle University was addressing and assessing every aspect of these new responsibilities.

Mention was made in several presentations that the new best practices may include more teaching opportunities for the researchers who are planning to become professors, but at the same time there will be increased efforts to help students shorten the duration of doctoral studies to three or three-and-one-half years. Tensions will arise, no doubt, among some of these conflicting goals. It is interesting to note that a recent five-year study to reassess doctoral students in the United States mirrors the tone of much that is being redesigned in the United Kingdom. "The Responsive Ph.D. states: [M]any critics have argued that doctoral education can't change. [This study] shows that doctoral education *must* change, *can* change, and is *already* changing in creative, effective ways."[23] That is perhaps a statement that will prove more true in the United Kingdom than it will in the United States, as some government funding in the United Kingdom is tied to best practices assessment.

Advice From Fulbright, Gates, and Marshall Experts

From the formal and informal conversations with directors of these programs, tips accrue, including the following:

Executive director of the U.K. Fulbright, Carol Madison Graham:

The Fulbright program in the U.K. is different from Marshall and perhaps others in that the panel is only interested in references from people who know the student's work. This means the student's professors and advisors. Therefore a letter from the Dean or President of the University and indeed the fellowship advisor is useless unless they have taught the student. However, each Fulbright program is different and where a statement from advisors could be useful if you know the student well is in Fulbright programs operating in countries where the cultural and political terrain is more difficult than it is in the United Kingdom. In these programs, your views might reassure the panel that the student can cope with or even thrive in a challenging environment. Always check their guidelines to be sure.

Advise your students to concentrate on their statements. It is very important for the student to be as clear as possible about the goal of the course of study he/she wishes to pursue. Otherwise it can appear that the scholarship is a way of achieving a position in life, and the Fulbright program is quite clear that we are not interested in people who want to BE something. We are interested in people who want to DO something.

Chairman of the Marshall Commission Jonathan Taylor addressed many important points. Emphasis was given to the following:

- Oral skills in the interview are extremely important qualities.
- Marshall/National Institute for Health partnerships are new developments over the last five years. The Marshall has new partnerships in the United Kingdom, with Birmingham, Belfast, and Nottingham, for example.
- The Marshall seeks diversity of scholarly applications beyond LSE/Oxford/Cambridge.
- Encourage applicants in Creative and Performing Arts—ballet, theatre, painting, film studies, even cartoons!
- Endorsement letters, whether signed by a provost, a dean, or an advisor, are important elements to be considered in the application process, but they are only one part of a complex picture that is created by the entire application.

Provost of the Gates Cambridge Trust, Dr. Gordon Johnson noted:

- A person should know what is on offer at Cambridge and research that information carefully. "Why do you want to come to Cambridge?" is a question that will be asked. The selection panel will press on how students know *this* is the place for them.
- Students must think through whether they are really qualified to take a place here because the right background is essential.

- Students must reason with themselves about how this opportunity fits in the longer term of their anticipated careers. A Gates Cambridge award is not a tip, a ribbon, or a trophy, but an opportunity to undertake further serious study and research.
- Cambridge academics (that is to say, the professors) must want the applicants. And they must be seen as people who will become leaders in the future in meaningful ways in their careers—in government, public, or private service. They may become engineers or scientists; they may work in applied fields, or industry, among many other careers. So they may be "quiet" leaders, but leaders nevertheless.
- Students should find professors with whom to work and have letters, if possible, from those professors within the application for Gates.
- Since the start of the program in 2001, 621 Gates Scholars from seventy-eight countries have taken up their awards, 265 from the United States of America. 382 Gates Scholars have completed the tenure of their scholarships as of Fall 2006.
- For the competition for entry in 2007, there were 632 applications for scholarships from students in the United States, 124 were interviewed in Annapolis and forty-eight scholarships were awarded. The Trust expects to make a further sixty new awards to students from countries other than the United States and these will be chosen from a field of applications of around 1,500.
- The revised Gates website (*http://www.gates.scholarships.cam.ac.uk*) will have additional information for the 2008 application and will incorporate the Scholars' website as well.

University of Oxford and the Rhodes Trust

At Oxford our conversations focused on graduate programs, new initiatives, courses, and developments in four divisions of the university: (1) social sciences; (2) mathematical, physical, and life sciences; (3) humanities; and (4) medical.[24] New skills training programs for graduate students who plan to enter teaching careers were explained. And more efforts will be made in some divisions for research done in the past solely by professors to now go forward *with* graduate assistants involved. Other points to note:

- New graduate degrees, such as an MST in Film Aesthetics and a new interdisciplinary medieval program, as well as a newly designed public policy degree focused on public service, add a fresh component to traditionally popular courses of study, such as International Relations.
- Collaboration with international academic and industrial partners is a central component of the academic program. For example, the National Institutes of Health at Bethesda, Maryland, are partnering with Oxford to provide an Oxford degree in biomedical science that is jointly supervised by PIs at both institutions. The M.D./Ph.D. program started in 2006. Marshall and Rhodes candidates are eligible to apply for this.
- Economics and engineering is a combined specialty that is popular. Many industries are interested in those graduates with bio-informatics, bio-nano sciences, and medical imaging degrees.
- In the *Times Higher Education Supplement* international comparisons of universities, Oxford ranks number three in the world, 2006–07.

A visit to Rhodes House and a conversation with the Warden of Rhodes House and Secretary to the Trust, Sir Colin Lucas, concluded the U.K. symposium. Points made during that conversation are paraphrased as follows:

- Students have opportunity through the Rhodes Scholarship to come to Oxford and transform themselves both through being fully engaged in their academic pursuits and through some other trait or characteristic (ambition to achieve, energy, cooperative pleasantness, strength of purpose, organization of time, etc.). Sports could teach these things, but not sports only. The point is that students must show a personal strength that allows them to overcome something and to achieve things. Natural talent is only part of it. How do they make the natural talent real and vibrant?

- The Rhodes Scholarship is about an ideal and it hopes to produce young people who will make a difference. Candidates must have a desire to do something and they must show concern for human beings. How will they make a difference? The candidates need a sense of how to achieve what they want to do.
- The Rhodes wants students who are really anchored inside, not just solid in the context of their own school. (Some have learned to package and sell themselves. Students who are just promoting themselves should not be encouraged to apply.)
- The Rhodes Committee wants students who have wider experience than just traveling, for example, to Zambia, to work in a laboratory in their own fields of study, as noble as that is. They need to be engaged outside their field as well.
- When working with the potential candidates on our campuses, consider putting the best students in groups with people who are unlike themselves. Give them mentors who have been in the world so that they may clarify why they are doing "this" and not "that." And if they have "a well-bred fury," it will be noticed.

What Have We Learned That Will Enhance Our Work as Advisors?

MODERN OR MEDIEVAL HOUSING

Having had a most enjoyable stay at Wolfson College, a modern college that opened in the 1960s and houses primarily graduate students,[25] NAFAns experienced firsthand that Cambridge consists not only of medieval spires but also of cosmopolitan campuses with all the necessary amenities. Although many American students choose to stay in the cloistered halls where ivy climbs the walls, students have a wide-ranging selection of colleges within which to live and find community.

EXEMPLARY STUDENTS

We visited with Gates, Rhodes, Fulbright, and Marshall Scholars and were inspired by them. It was exhilarating to realize that every student we met was maximizing his or her time abroad. Yes, they had experienced challenges. Yes, they had had to extend themselves to make new friends and adjust academically and culturally. A detailed printed response of Marshall Scholars on their research experience confirms both the dynamic and enriching part of their time in the United Kingdom as well as the reality that "self-discipline is crucial."[26] Several students at Wolfson chortled about the small adjustments and spoke with passion about the large ones, citing as small but puzzling why the British would have one spigot for cold water and one for hot water in every sink. One Gates international relations Ph.D. student responded memorably, "Here you don't just have to figure out the answers. Sometimes you have to figure out the questions. We understand that the opportunities we have here are not about 'the two taps.'"

FUNDING

All of us have had students among the "worthy many" whom we believe deserved the chance to study in Britain but did not win the scholarship of their dreams. Realizing that there is never enough scholarship money and that the monies available are not easy to find, still we came away knowing that, beyond the major foundations, almost every university acknowledged that it had some financial discretion to fund some graduate students from abroad. It is worth investigating for funding at the university of your student's choice and not a hopeless cause.[27]

BRITISH COUNCIL USA RESOURCES

NAFAns have many resources through our listserve, our archive, and our bulletin board discussions. We also have constantly updated resources through the British Council USA. For example, *http://www.britishcouncil.org/usa-education-graduate-degree.htm#*. This is the graduate website—and the FAQ section has an option to contact a staff member with a specific question! What a great service to add to this fine resource—human beings with answers who will respond to our enquiries. Additionally, the website has a glossary at *http://www.britishcouncil.org/usa-education-uk-glossary.htm*. The site explains, for example, that a "college" in the United Kingdom sense is not used interchangeably with "university." Its first definition is "a residential community like a dormitory (collegiate systems are found at the Universities of Oxford, Cambridge, and Durham)."

A Cautionary Tale about our Applicants' Strength of Purpose

In spring of 2007 many NAFA members read the opinion piece written by two Rhodes Scholars and posted to *The Harvard Crimson,* titled "Oxford Blues."[28] The students evaluate and find wanting not only the advisement system at Harvard after winning the Rhodes, but also the Oxford library system, the academic experience there, the funds they are provided, the food, the night-life, and many other aspects of their Oxford experience. They conclude: "Do not apply for the Rhodes unless you are ready to study and live in Oxford."

Eliot Gerson, the American secretary for the Rhodes, taking great exception to the students' characterization of the experience, responded with insightful information for advisors and potential applicants. He addresses four central challenges that students must face no matter what course of study they plan to follow when entering Oxford, three of which are transitions—(1) to graduate work, (2) to a very different university system, and (3) from one country to another—"also quite different despite the common language." His last point seems particularly one that scholarship advisors might find difficult but essential to communicate clearly to students: "[F]inally, they have high expectations of themselves but may not always realize that others also have those expectations of them."

Two additional points in the secretary's letter seem central to our work as NAFA and as advisors on our own campuses:

- Dr. Gerson counters the students' view of the Oxford experience by noting "there are now more American Rhodes Scholars choosing to remain at Oxford for the full three years of Rhodes financial support (rather than one or two) than at any time in our hundred-year plus history."
- Having recognized that Oxford demands "strength of purpose" that some winners may not have, he concludes: "Their article suggests that Oxford was not the optimal place for either, which is regrettable, and clearly it is not right for everyone, as we never tire of advising—but that is unlikely to have been Oxford's (or Harvard's) fault."

Thus we are encouraged to have conversations that are as focused and frank as possible with our best and brightest applicants. By doing so, as they investigate which course of study at which institution they wish to pursue, our students may also confront themselves and grow wiser about their own identity and strength of purpose.

Blue Fire at Cambridge

This essay has been borne on the wings of a bird I saw the evening before the NAFA conference began. I was standing on a bridge over the Cam with Suzanne McCray, listening to the King's College Choir crooning "Blue Moon" kinds of songs as they stood in punts in the river. I was also savoring the realization that back home in Texas it was twenty-five degrees hotter than it was in cool Cambridge. From the vantage point of the bridge I could survey on one side the people relaxing on the grass against the backdrop of King's College and enjoy on the other side a pasture full of black and white Holstein cows that seemed to be swaying with the beat. Life was good. Then over my head, a small, fast iridescent-blue something flew, flashed, and whirred into a chestnut tree at the river's edge. The English student beside us explained that we had just seen a kingfisher. A kingfisher! Nothing I had read by Hopkins or seen in a Van Gogh painting had prepared me. To use Seamus Heaney's phrase, such moments "catch the heart off-guard and blow it open."

That electric-blue bird has become emblematic of something about the trip for me, but I am not certain exactly what. Maybe it was the astonishing array of fine programs presented to us. Maybe it was the beauty of Cambridge. Maybe it was emblematic of the great good companionship of fellow travelers from NAFA who lift one another's spirits over and over again. Or maybe I equate what I felt upon seeing that fire-filled, magical bird with all those students whose earnest efforts to reach for the stars lift my spirit right with them to the sky. Auden spoke of "points of light" that flame out wherever the just exchange their messages. My variation on that, built upon kingfishers, would be imaging little blue flames in all our offices at all our schools where NAFA members work with the students they believe in on tasks that are worth the doing. They are coaching and celebrating and crying and sending out fire.

In Appreciation

Sir David Williams, QC, DL, vice-chancellor emeritus of Cambridge, welcomed us to Cambridge the first evening. He emphasized the close relationship between the United States and Britain and spoke graciously of many vital qualities he associated with our homeland. He concluded his reflections by thanking Dr. Gordon Johnson for his excellent work with the Gates Cambridge scheme and noted that Dr. Johnson had been a leader in keeping the vitality of exchange between the United States and United Kingdom in the modern era. We, too, are indebted to Dr. Johnson for his long-standing and enthusiastic support of NAFA. We are also grateful for the support provided by the Gates Cambridge Trust during our symposium.

Notes

Chapter One: Recognizing and Challenging Our Colleges'
Most Outstanding Students by Richard J. Light

1. Below is a list of the questions asked of the graduating class of 2007.

Why did you choose to come to Harvard?

What is the best part of your academic experience so far? Please give a very specific answer.

Is there a very specific disappointment academically that you have had in the first semester? What is it?

Did this experience give you any ideas for avoiding disappointment in the future?

On a 1–10 scale, where 10 is really great, how would you rate your overall academic happiness here as we approach the end of freshman year? And— slightly different question—on that 1–10 scale, how would you rate your personal happiness freshman year? (If the numbers are very different, ask why.)

Approximately how many hours a week would you honestly estimate that you study, outside of sitting in your classes?

Do you have any clear sense of how hard you work, compared with friends or acquaintances you might have at other excellent colleges?

In general, do you believe the academic pressures and your sheer academic workload here at Harvard is more than, less than, or pretty much the same as, what your friends at other colleges are experiencing? Any examples?

Do you like the way our first year advising system is organized? If yes, please say why. If no, please say why not. And if you don't like the current system, do you have any practical ideas for how Harvard might strengthen it?

If you could add or change one or two questions on the freshman housing questionnaire, what would you suggest?

Is there a single course that you would say "profoundly affected you" in your first semester here? If yes, what was it, and more important, why was it so profoundly effective? Please focus on substance of a course, or its organization, or the way it was taught, or the instructor's teaching style, rather than just "the instructor was a nice guy."

Some faculty members make it entirely clear, throughout their course (especially in social sciences and humanities courses), what their politics and personal opinions are. They pretty much wear their personal views on their sleeve, publicly. Other faculty members cover material and never reveal their personal views about the material. Which of these two strategies do you believe is more effective in engaging you in classes? Which teaching strategy do you think leads to your learning more?

Think of the courses you have taken so far. In the process of taking them, can you think of an example where taking a class has led you to change your mind about something? If you believe that a goal of college is to encourage students to think and "rethink" their views about many topics, what do you believe is the most effective ways for faculty to help this to happen?

Have you had some particular interactions outside of classes with your fellow students that actually have led you to change your mind about something? If you are comfortable, could you briefly say what it was and what led you to change?

Do you feel you are a member of any small community here on campus? What is it? (if yes)—do you believe being part of this small community is a critical ingredient that makes you feel "part of this place"? Or is it just a pleasure to be involved and it doesn't lead to any "broader" sense of belonging?

Are you involved with the same, main extracurricular activity(ies) that you planned and anticipated before you arrived at Harvard? If no, why? If yes, are you getting out of it (or them) what you hoped?

As you think ahead to next year, can you identify one, specific thing you will do differently on campus, because of what you learned from your experience freshman year? Why? Please explain.

Have you thought about taking a year off, either before coming here or perhaps sometime during the next three years? If you are taking a future year off, have your experiences here at Harvard affected your decision in some specific way? If yes, what might you do and why?

What is the single best bit of advice you got during freshman year? Who gave it to you? Why was it so helpful?

What advice do you wish you had gotten at the beginning of freshman year that you didn't get?

You have now been here one full semester. If your best friend a year behind you in high school had just learned he or she has been admitted here and is planning to come next year, what would you tell her to do in the next nine months that would enhance her overall happiness and success here?

In retrospect, looking back on freshman year near the end of the year, what if anything, regardless of advice from others, would you have done differently, academically?

In retrospect, looking back on freshman year, what if anything would you have done differently, with nonacademic parts of your life here?

In your own experience and looking at your friends, do you consider the workload and lifestyle in math/science courses different from the workload in humanities and social science courses here? If yes, has this affected the courses you have taken, and will take in the future?

Do you feel well enough informed to choose a concentration wisely? Are there one or two key factors influencing your choice? What are they?

Have you met anyone in your concentration? Did what he or she told you influence you? If yes, how?

Do you have summer plans yet? What are they? If yes, why did you choose to do this? Do your summer plans link in any specific way with your academic or extracurricular interests at college? If yes, how?

If you needed a recommendation from a faculty member or teaching fellow (TF) for a summer job, or internship, or fellowship, do you have a specific person whom you could ask and whom you believe knows you well enough? If yes, would it be a regular faculty member? A TF? An advisor?

How many times have you met for a chat with a regular faculty member one-on-one (not a teaching fellow) during fall semester of freshman year? How about spring semester so far? Any faculty member? This does not count e-mail—the question is about a real meeting.

If you took a freshman seminar, was it a good experience? Can you be specific about why yes, or why no? We don't need to know names of instructors, just about your experience, and why it was good or not so good.

For your personal learning, and engagement with the substantive, academic material, do you find that small classes (twenty or fewer) are significantly different from larger classes? Why or why not?

Suppose a dean proposed that every freshman had to take two small classes (twenty or smaller) each semester in first year. Do you think if that were implemented, your academic or personal experience here during freshman year would have been significantly different?

There are two different ways a student can sit in a small class. One is where the entire class is small, with a small total enrollment (e.g., under twenty). The second situation is where a very large course, such as basic economics, divides students into small sections that meet regularly, often led by a TF. Do you consider these two experiences similar or different in a major way? If different, could you please briefly say why?

Have you done any volunteer work yet, even though you are still new here? If yes, what impact has that volunteer work had for you, personally?

Do you have any major, outside-of-class extracurricular commitments right now? If yes, what impact have such commitments had for you, personally?

How important is the active practice of your religion to you? Do you believe that outside of classes you have ample opportunities to practice your religion if you choose to?

Do you feel you have gotten to learn new things about other religions since you arrived on campus? If yes, has what you learned changed your view about other religions? Please be honest—we are not looking for "politically correct" answers, just honest answers.

Do you believe since you arrived on campus that you have personally re-thought your own religious convictions? If it isn't too personal, if your answer is yes, has this re-thinking led you to strengthen and reaffirm your beliefs, or to question them more than you expected?

Do you find that your classes in humanities and social sciences include, or avoid, or are quite neutral about topics that connect with religion? If you happen to have an example, whether it is positive or negative in your view, please feel free to share it briefly.

Do you ever feel inhibited, in any way, about discussing religion or religious perspectives, "out loud" in any of your classes? If yes, is that because you feel the professor would not welcome it, or is it more just personally uncomfortable for you?

You will soon be choosing some of your fellow students to live with for next year as a group. Do you consider the current blocking process a good one? If you feel strongly you would change it, what one change might you recommend?

The word "diversity" usually is used to describe racial and ethnic diversity. Yet as an increasingly globalized college and university, Harvard has students from a variety of religions. Some are deeply religious and other are entirely nonreligious, with lots in the middle. Do you feel you have learned about other religions during freshman year? If yes, did that learning take place in classes, or in more informal settings such as dorms or extracurricular activities? Please don't give a "politically correct" answer—we really want to know!

Potential Options for Students (especially first year students)

We all know some students who are very smart and thoughtful, yet are shy or hesitant to speak up in class. If voluntary sessions were offered to undergraduates to help them develop more comfort, and provide them with an opportunity to offer some specific suggestions that would help them to speak up more in class—do you think such sessions should be offered?

Would you go to two or three such sessions, designed to encourage more students to feel comfortable speaking up regularly in classes, and taking some risks in classes to express your views, even when you are uncertain your view or answer is the "right" one or the one that the professor expects?

Very few students have worked in "study groups" outside of classes when they went to high school. If Harvard were to offer a voluntary two- or three-session workshop in how to study productively together in small groups, outside of classes, would you sign up to participate in such an opportunity?

At some of the graduate schools here at Harvard, such as the business school and the law school and the Kennedy School, students are asked to speak in class regularly. Sometimes class contributions even count toward a student's grade in a course, thereby encouraging each person to contribute and to occasionally take risks by speaking up. Do you wish there were some such policy here for undergraduates at the College also? Why or why not?

Impressions about Faculty Members

Do you find that faculty here, the ones you have met or seen so far, welcome a diverse set of views about the topics they teach? In other words, are faculty members you have been exposed to so far happy to entertain and discuss views from the political left and right, from religious and secular students—from many different perspectives?

If there is one specific example that stands out in your mind of a faculty member who did welcome different perspectives, how did this happen? You don't need to mention the professor's name, just tell what happened.

If there is one specific example that stands out in your mind of a faculty member who did not welcome different perspectives, how did this happen? Again, no names needed, just tell what happened.

If you were advising the president of the university, and the dean of Harvard College and the dean of freshmen about a single, constructive change they could make that would be a great change—even if you are very happy here now—can you think of a single, concrete change to suggest that is realistic and practical? Please be as specific as possible. Pretend you are "dean for a day."

As you know, the deans and faculty for Harvard College are beginning to review the curriculum for the College for the first time in many years. Are there one or two major suggestions you would make if you were in charge of that curriculum review? Again, pretend that you are "dean for a day."

What is the biggest surprise that you have experienced since you arrived here one semester ago?

One of the goals of college, for all students, is to grow and mature personally in certain nonacademic ways, to learn more about yourself, to see others in new ways. Do you believe that in your first year here, you have grown in any such ways? If your answer is yes, could you give just one, specific example of a new perspective, a kind of personal growth, that you believe you have experienced here at the College?

Are you the sort of person who sets realistic goals for yourself as you look forward to the coming weeks and months? In the context of being here at the College, do you have one or two specific goals? Please share them if you are comfortable, together with why they are important to you.

My final question is, sometimes when being interviewed both at Harvard and at other colleges, students say they found the time a good investment because it got them to think about some things they might not otherwise have thought about. Did you find that just the process of doing this interview got you thinking about certain ideas or topics that you might not otherwise have thought about?

Chapter Two: Connecting Undergraduate Research Programs with Fellowship Advising by Laura Damuth

1. This article is based on a presentation given at the 2005 Louisville NAFA conference by Laura Damuth, University of Nebraska–Lincoln and Nichole Fazio, University of Washington.

Chapter Three: Marshalling Service by Mary Denyer

1. Website references for the projects mentioned include:
   http://www.marshallscholarship.org/msvp/
   http://www.marshallscholarship.org/kpl/
   http://www.millatschoolsfund.org/
   http://www.aidemocracy.org/
   http://www.oxfordgatehouse.org/
   http://www.thebritishmuseum.ac.uk/jobs/volunteering.html
   http://www.researchersinresidence.ac.uk/rir/
   http://www.asylum-welcome.supanet.com/

Chapter Five: Student Ambassadors in the Age of Anti-Americanism by Carol Madison Graham

1. The attitude of "I'll be fine because I disagree with U.S. policy" is one that Americans in the Middle East used with justification for some time. They were therefore unprepared when anti-Americanism cum anti-Westernism became ascendant. As a diplomat in Lebanon in the 1980s I tried in vain to explain to the residents that things had changed—that the Islamic fundamentalist terrorists had a different agenda. Eventually most of them got the message (from the fundamentalists) and left. I believe the same is now true for other parts of the world and especially the United Kingdom with regard to anti-Americanism.

2. U.S. students know less geography than students in other countries. Surveys show that U.S. students' geography knowledge ranks far below students in such countries as Japan, the United Kingdom, Germany, and Canada. Even worse, geographical knowledge has declined over the years so now many children cannot read maps or locate state, cities, or important physical features, even in the United States. This lack of geographical knowledge is more than an embarrassment; it is a threat to our country's status as a world leader. From website of the National Council for Geographic Education.

Chapter Seven: Helping Faculty Write Better Recommendation Letters by Joe Schall

1. Selecting from the wide variety of publications on recommendation letter writing, I choose the following ten as the most seminal articles that collectively provide readers with scope for the subject. Henry Rosovsky and Matthew Harley, *Evaluation and the Academy: Are We Doing the Right Thing?* (Cambridge, MA.). American Academy of Arts and Sciences: 2002: 26. William Cole, "By Rewarding Mediocrity We Discourage Excellence," *The Chronicle of Higher Education* (January 6, 1993): B1–2. Stephen Ceci and Douglas Peters, "Letters of Reference: A Naturalistic Study of the Effects of Confidentiality," *American Psychologist 39* (1) (1984): 29–31. Jennie Farley, "Academic Recommendations: Males and Females as Judges and Judged," *AAUP Bulletin* (May 1978): 82–85. Eric R. Landrum, "Student Expectations of Grade Inflation," *Journal of Research and Development in Education* 32(2) (1999): 124–28. Paul K. Kasambira, "Recommendation Inflation," *Teacher Educator 20*(2) (1984): 26–29. "Collecting Letters of Recommendation: Can This Process Be Saved?" *The Chronicle of Higher Education* (April 5, 2002), *http://chronicle.com/*. Megan Rooney, "Texas Tech Professor's Policy on Student Recommendations Prompts Federal Inquiry," *The Chronicle of Higher Education* (February 21, 2003). *http://chronicle.com/*. Kristen Precht, "A Cross-Cultural Comparison of Letters of Recommendation," *English for Specific Purposes 17*(3) (1998): 241–55. Family Educational Rights and Privacy Act. Code of Federal Regulations, Title 34, Volume 1, Parts 1 to 299, *http://www.deltabravo.net/custody/ferpa.htm*. A useful discussion on the subject from a sociological perspective also appears in a section of Sissela Bok's *Lying: Moral Choice in Public and Private Life* (New York: Vintage Books 1999), 326.

2. The second edition of *Writing Recommendation Letters: A Faculty Handbook* is available from Phoenix Direct, 877-398-7485. The author can be contacted at 814-63-6077 or *schall@ems.psu.edu*.

3. See for example, the following articles. "Collecting Letters of Recommendation: Can This Process be Saved?" *The Chronicle of Higher Education* (April 5, 2002), *http://chronicle.com/*. James M. Lang, "The Academic Pyramid Club," *The Chronicle of Higher Education* (January 23, 2004), *http://chronicle.com/*. Alison Schneider, "Bias in the Ivory Tower: An Unintended Consequence of the Buckley Amendment for Graduate Admissions?" *Journal of Applied Psychology 66*(1) (2000): 7–11. A. Gerson Greenburg, Jennifer Doyle, and D.K. McClure, "Letters of Recommendation for Surgical Residencies: What They Say and What They Mean," *Journal of Surgical Research 56* (1994): 192–98.

4. Vincent Kiernan, "If You Like This Student, Click Here," *The Chronicle of Higher Education* (June 4, 2004), *http://chronicle.com/*. Megan Rooney, "Texas Tech Professor's Policy on Student Recommendations Prompts

Federal Inquiry," *The Chronicle of Higher Education* (February 21, 2003), *http://chronicle.com/*. Alison Schneider, "Why You Can't Trust Letters of Recommendation," *The Chronicle of Higher Education* (June 30, 2000): A14–6. Deirdre McCloskey, "The Random Insanity of Letters of Recommendation," *The Chronicle of Higher Education* (March 1, 2002), *http://chronicle.com/*. William Cole, "By Rewarding Mediocrity We Discourage Excellence," *The Chronicle of Higher Education* (January 6, 1993): B1–2. Daniel Callahan, "When Friendship Calls, Should Truth Answer?" *The Chronicle of Higher Education* (August 7, 1978): 32.

5. Michael Ryan and David L. Martinson, "Perceived Effects of Exaggeration in Recommendation Letters," *Journalism & Mass Communication Educator* (Spring 2000): 40–52. Stephen Ceci and Douglas Peters, "Letters of Reference: A Naturalistic Study of the Effects of Confidentiality," *American Psychologist, 39* (1) (1984): 29–31. Jennie Farley, "Academic Recommendations: Males and Females as Judges and Judged," *AAUP Bulletin* (May 1978) 82–85. Frances Trix and Carolyn Psenka, "Exploring the Color of Glass: Letters of Recommendation for Female and Male Medical Faculty," *Discourse and Society 14*(2) (2003): 191–220. Jule Henderson, John Briere, and Ross Hartsough, "Sexism and Sex Roles in Letters of Recommendation to Graduate Training in Psychology," *Canadian Psychology 21*(2) (1980): 75–79. Susan E. Bell, C. Suzanne Cole, and Lilliane Floge, "Letters of Recommendation in Academe: Do Women and Men Write in Different Languages?" *The American Sociologist* (1992): 7–22. Eric R. Landrum, "Student Expectations of Grade Inflation," *Journal of Research and Development in Education 32*(2) (1999): 124–28. Ruth Stevens, "Proposals Presented to Curb Grade Inflation," *Princeton Weekly Bulletin 93*(24) (April 12, 2004), *http://www.princeton.edu/pr/pwb/04/0419/1b.shtml*. Ruth Stevens, "Faculty Approves Proposals to Establish Grading Standard," *Princeton Weekly Bulletin 93*(26) (May 5, 2004), *http://www.princeton.edu/pr/pwb/04/0503/*. G. Siskind, "Mine Eyes Have Seen a Host of Angels," *American Psychologist 21* (1966): 804–806. Paul K. Kasambira, "Recommendation Inflation," *Teacher Educator 20*(2) (1984): 26–29. Stephen M. Colarelli, Regina Hechanova-Alampay, and Kristophor G. Canali, "Letters of Recommendation: An Evolutionary Psychological Perspective," *Human Relations 55*(3) (2002): 315–44. George W. Tommasi, Karen B. Williams, and Cynthia R. Nordstrom, "Letters of Recommendation: What Information Captures HR Professionals' Attention?" *Journal of Business and Psychology 13* (1) (Fall 1998): 5–18. Sherwood H. Peres and J. Robert Garcia, "Validity and Dimensions of Descriptive Adjectives Used in Reference Letters for Engineering Applicants," *Personnel Psychology 15* (1962): 279–86.

6. Henry Rosovsky and Matthew Harley, *Evaluation and the Academy: Are We Doing the Right Thing?* (Cambridge, MA.), American Academy of Arts and Sciences (2002): 26.

7. Frank Evans Berkheimer, *A Scale for the Evaluation of School Administrators' Letters of Recommendation for Teachers* (Master of Science thesis, Pennsylvania State College, State College, PA 1936), 45.

8. Lloyd N. Morrisett, *Letters of Recommendation: A Study of Letters of Recommendation as an Instrument in the Selection of Secondary School Teachers* (New York: College Press, 205. Originally presented as the author's thesis, Columbia University, NY. 1935.

9. I have found a number of tactics to be especially valuable when presenting student cases. Simply supplying photographs of students next to the text describing their cases humanizes the cases for faculty. Planting specific references to the school where the faculty members work makes the material more relevant. Finally, making certain that the case text involves some minor, manageable ethical dilemma for the faculty members—while setting the condition that they do want to help the student involved in the case—promotes thoughtful debate.

10. Having faculty share their sentences and paragraphs aloud with other groups after internal group discussion is highly recommended.

11. James M. Lang, "The Academic Pyramid Club," *The Chronicle of Higher Education* (January 23, 2004), *http://chronicle.com/*. Daniel Callahan, "When Friendship Calls, Should Truth Answer?" *Chronicle of Higher Education* (August 7, 1978), 32.

12. See note 3.

13. *The Teaching Professor* is available from Magna Publications, 2718 Dryden Dr., Madison, WI 53704. Phone: 608-246-3590. Website: *http://www.smu.ca/administration/oid/the_teaching_professor.htm.*

14. See note 6.

15. See note 2.

Chapter Eight: International Students: A Case for More Advisor Support by Camille Stillwell

1. The annual publication of *Open Doors* is available through IIE. The data in this paragraph as well as additional information on international students in the United States is available at *http://opendoors.iienetwork.org/page/89251/; jsessionid=337hbflpj38at.*

Chapter Eleven: Why Visit the United Kingdom: Confession of a Journeyman Fellowship Advisor by Mark Bauer

1. I was much relieved to read in the *Guardian* recently that the 2008 RAE will not be scrapped after all. This looks like the last time the RAE will be configured as it is currently. The plan is to go to a metric-based rather than peer-reviewed assessment, which will work fine for the sciences but not at all

fine for the humanities. We'll see. For more information on the 2001 and 2008 RAE visit the program's website at *http://hero.ac.uk/rae/*.

2. See *The Times Good University Guide* for its 2007 league table: *http://www.timesonline.co.uk/tol/life_and_style/education/good_university_guide./The Guardian* also provides an interactive league table online: *http://education.guardian.co.uk/universityguide2006*. For information on the Quality Assurance Assessment, see *http://www.qaa.ac.uk/*.

3. We were extremely fortunate in visiting Edinburgh and St. Andrews in June, when the long days are lovely. But this lovely season is particularly short so far north. Students from Alaska, Maine, or even Seattle may have no trouble adjusting to the long grey winter, but for other students the lack of sun can be a challenge. That said, the Scottish universities make a virtue of their relative isolation by encouraging participation in a particularly lively and engaging array of student activities.

4. For more detailed information garnered from our two NAFA study trips, I can do no better than to point the reader to Paula Warrick's wonderful notes from our 2004 U.K. visit. These notes can be found on the NAFA bulletin board at: *http://www.nafadvisors.org/board/message.php?id=159&highlight=159*; or search by "Warrick" or "U.K. and Ireland." I also want to refer readers to "Keys to the United Kingdom," Betsy Vardaman's very helpful account of what we learned from the 2002 U.K. trip. This article may be found in *Beyond Winning: National Scholarship Competitions and the Student Experience,* the proceedings of the NAFA 2003 conference.

5. The Goodenough Club is associated with Goodenough College and is located in central London, provides "faculty accommodations for universities, the professions and charities." See *http://www.club.goodenough.ac.uk/*.

Chapter 13: Coin of the Realm: Graduate Education in Britain by Elizabeth Vardaman

1. Participating NAFA representatives were American University, University of Arkansas, University of Arizona, Baylor University, Carnegie Mellon University, Columbia University, DePauw University, Florida State University, Grinnell College, Illinois at Chicago, University of Kentucky, University of Louisville, Loyola Marymount University, University of Maryland, Baltimore County, University of Maryland, University of Massachusetts at Amherst, Muhlenberg College, University of Nevada–Reno, Northwestern University, North Carolina State, University of Notre Dame, Ohio University, Ohio State University, Penn State, University of Pittsburg, Pomona College, Santa Clara University, Seattle University, U.S. Air Force Academy, U.S. Coast Guard Academy, Vanderbilt University, Villanova University, Western Kentucky University, University of Washington, and University of William & Mary.

2. Participating U.K. universities and funding institutions: administrators and faculty members from Cambridge University; the Courtauld Institute; Imperial College London; London School of Economics and Political Science; University College London; Royal Holloway, University of London; University of Manchester; School of Oriental and African Studies; Cardiff University; Newcastle University; University of Sussex, Institute of Development Studies; University of Bradford; London School of Hygiene and Tropical Medicine; Jonathan Taylor, chairman of the Marshall Commission; Gordon Johnson, provost of the Gates Cambridge Trust; Carol Madison Graham, executive director of the U.K. Fulbright; Mary Denyer, alumni officer, Marshall Commission; Tracy Jesty from British Council; and Gates, Fulbright, and Marshall Scholars.

3. Planning Committee: Dr. Gordon Johnson, president of Wolfson College, Cambridge University; Elizabeth Vardaman, co-chair, Baylor University; Jane Morris, co-chair, Villanova University; Mark Bauer, Yale University; Ann Brown, Ohio University; Suzanne McCray, University of Arkansas; John Richardson, University of Louisville; Paula Warrick, American University; and Susan Whitbourne, University of Massachusetts at Amherst.

4. Effort has been made to assure accuracy in the reports on universities. The presenters, from whom some materials were paraphrased, include: (1) Professor John King, Transport and Shipping Research Group of Cardiff Business School, and Miss Sandra Elliott, director of International Development, (2) Professor Mary Ritter, pro-rector for Postgraduate and International Affairs at Imperial College, (3) Mr. Jethro Pettit, research officer on the Participation, Power and Social Change Team at IDS, (4) Professor Joanna Lewis, lecturer in International History and by Ms. Catherine Baldwin, head of Recruitment and Admissions at LSE, (5) Professor Sharon Huttly, dean of Studies at London School of Hygiene and Tropical Medicine, (6) Dr. Jim Whitman, director of the M.A. program Department of Peace Studies at University of Bradford, (7) Professor Peter Robb, pro-director for Research and Professor of the History of India from SOAS, and (8) Professor Stuart Turley, associate dean for Graduate Education and Ms. Tanya Luff of International Development from University of Manchester. Other presenters are referenced directly within the text for specific attributions. Any errors in fact or interpretation would be deeply regretted and solely the responsibility of the author.

5. The six schools are (1) Arts and Humanities, (2) Biological Sciences, (3) Clinical Medicine, (4) Humanities and Social Sciences, (5) Physical Sciences, and (6) Technology and Management. See *http://www.admin.cam.ac.uk/univ/gsprospectus/subjects/* for details of which subjects fit within each school.

6. Some of the material presented in the section on University of Cambridge was provided by Dr. Kate Pretty, pro-vice-chancellor and by Ms. Louise Burton, head of Graduate Admissions, Board of Graduate Studies.

I am indebted to Gordon Johnson for clarification of many aspects of this process as well.

7. Dr. Johnson added, "The Board does have a role greater than that of letter-box, however, and it may, in some very rare case, question a decision or send it back to the Degree Committee."

8. The RAE is the national scrutiny procedure conducted by the Higher Education Funding Council for evaluating the quality of University research. Scores of 5* indicate a majority of subject areas in a department have reached levels of international excellence.

9. Some materials provided are drawn from the presentation for the Courtauld by Professor Mignon Nixon and have been verified by Professor Nixon.

10. From Courtauld Graduate Prospectus found online at *http:// www. courtauld.ac.uk/prospectivestudents/courses2007/pg/researchdegrees.html.*

11. New programs for 2007 include M.A. in Development Studies, M.A. in Poverty and Development, M.A. in Science, Society and Development. M.Phil. in Development studies (a two-year program) newly revised.

12. Taken from Institute of Development Studies portfolio of literature for 2007 programs.

13. A white paper on this topic, "Doctoral Training in the U.K.," was presented by Professor Ella Ritchie, Pro-Vice-Chancellor for Teaching and Learning at Newcastle University and is referenced later in this article.

14. An extended list of research themes and projects: *http://www. bradford.ac.uk/acad/peace/tmp/groups/#1.*

15. This assessment is based on materials provided by Professor Francis Robinson of Royal Holloway, president of the Royal Asiatic Society, who spoke to us on "Islam and Modernity." He also noted that University of Edinburgh's Dept. of Islamic and Middle Eastern Studies was the only 5* department for research in the 2001 Research Assessment Exercise.

16. A unique feature is that a student can go through an entire program in one region because of the breadth/depth across regions of the world at SOAS. Seventy masters degrees, such as M.A. in Japanese Literature, M.A. in Sinology, M.A. in Turkish Studies, are listed in the literature.

17. Some material in the overview of University College London was provided by Professor Jan Atkinson, pro-provost for North America and professor of Psychology and co-director of the inspirational Visual Development Unit, located at *http://www.psychol.ucl.ac.uk/vdu/index.html.*

18. The Woodrow Wilson National Fellowship Foundation has completed a five-year initiative begun in 2000, titled "The Responsive Ph.D.," that offers a range of recommendations for American doctoral education.

19. "The Changing Face of the Doctorate," *The Independent,* January 18, 2007. On-line at *http://education.independent.co.uk/graduate_options/ article2160679.ece* (viewed Feb. 1, 2007).

20. Professor Ella Ritchie, presentation at NAFA Symposium at Wolfson and white paper on "Doctoral Training in the United Kingdom," June 28, 2006.

21. Dr. Chris Park, "Redefining the Doctorate," a discussion paper produced by The Higher Education Academy, January 2007. In this impressive study, Park quotes J. Nyquist (2002) "The Ph.D.: A Tapestry of Change for the 21st Century." *Change* (Nov/Dec): 12–20, whose insight I have also quoted.

22. Ritchie, "Doctoral Training in the United Kingdom," 2.

23. Woodrow Wilson National Fellowship Foundation, executive summary for "The Responsive Ph.D.: Innovations in University Doctoral Education."

24. Presentations were made for social sciences by Professor Neil MacFarlane, head of department, Politics and International Relations; for mathematical, physical, and life sciences by Dr. Robert Taylor of the Physics Division; for humanities by Ms. Joanna Innes, director of Graduate Studies in History; and for the medical division by Professor Nick Rawlins, Watts Professor of Psychology. The program was arranged by James Tibbert of the Student Funding and International Office.

25. The college has a limited number of mature students studying for a first degree, but Wolfson has never taken students straight from school.

26. Many thanks to Mary Denyer of the Marshall Commission for providing us a white paper on "Marshall Scholar Experiences of Research in the United Kingdom." This helpful overview of comments from Marshall Scholars has been scanned and will be posted to the NAFA website.

27. The ORS awards scheme is designed to attract high quality research students to U.K. universities. The awards are open to overseas students undertaking a research degree and may be held in any field of study. Each award covers the difference between the tuition fee for a U.K./E.U. graduate student and that chargeable to an overseas graduate student.

28. "Oxford Blues," by Melissa L. Dell and Swati Mylavarapu, *The Harvard Crimson*, February 25, 2007, *http://www.thecrimson.com/ article. aspx?ref=517274*.

Index